FIRST THE DESERT

THEN…..

THE DESSERT!!

By: Jerry A. Roff

Copyright (c) 2011 by Jerry A. Roff

First The Desert, Then The Dessert
By Jerry A. Roff

Printed In the United States of America

ISBN: 978-0-578-08431-2

All rights reserved soley by the author. The author guarantees all Content are original and do not infringe upon the legal rights of any other person or work. No part of this book may be reproduced in any form without written permission of the author.

Unless otherwise indicated, Bible quotations are taken from The New International version of the Bible.

For more information about the ministry of Jerry A. Roff go to: www.firehousechurch.us or www.increasingfire.us
net

CONTENTS

Dedication
Introduction

Chapter 1	The Promises of God
Chapter 2	Why The Desert?
Chapter 3	Humility Before Honor
Chapter 4	To Be Tested
Chapter 5	To Teach You
Chapter 6	Faith
Chapter 7	Trust
Chapter 8	Persistence
Chapter 9	How To Respond in the Desert
Chapter 10	Dessert in the Desert
Chapter 11	Finally, The Dessert

Dedication: The Bible says in **Proverbs 18:22** *"He who* finds a wife finds a good *thing,* And obtains favor from the LORD." *(NKJV)*

Next to my Savior and Lord Jesus, my wife Charlotte is the best thing that has happened to me. I honor her in the writing of this book. For she has walked with me through the desert and is with me experiencing the dessert! I thank you for the love and faithfulness you show to our Lord as well as the love and faithfulness you give to your family, and everyone you come in contact with. I have never known anyone as compassionate and giving as you. I thank God for you Charlotte. I thank God for your life, love and support. The greatest thing in all of life's journeys is that we have been through them all "together". You are my "Endless Love". I thank God for the 30 years of marriage we celebrate June 20th of this year as well!

I dedicate this book as well to our daughters Jeanette, Jenna and Jillian. Jeanette, I look forward to the day we meet again in Heaven. Jenna and Jillian, I pray that you live life to the fullest, and lead many to Christ as you fulfill God's destiny for you life.

I also want to thank our church family at The Fire House Church that have stuck with us, and for all of their love, prayers and support during our several year recent desert experience. 'Thank You"!

Introduction:

DT 8:1 *Be careful to follow every command I am giving you today, so that you may live and increase and may enter and possess the land that the LORD promised on oath to your forefathers. 2 Remember how the LORD your God led you all the way in the desert these forty years, to humble you and to test you in order to know what was in your heart, whether or not you would keep his commands. 3 He humbled you, causing you to hunger and then feeding you with manna, which neither you nor your fathers had known, to teach you that man does not live on bread alone but on every word that comes from the mouth of the LORD. 4 Your clothes did not wear out and your feet did not swell during these forty years.*

Have you ever wondered why in life we often go through what we call "Desert" or "Wilderness" Experiences? Those times where it appears we are alone. It seems like God is not hearing or answering or providing. Those painful times where we may be spiritually dry.

We are God's children. We are to be blessed of God, favored of God, prosperous and "More than Conquerors".
Yet we experience those times in our lives when it appears our life is anything but blessed, or prosperous.

We believe and know that *"God knows the plans He has for us. Plans not to harm us but to prosperous us, to give us a hope and a future."* **(Jeremiah 29:11)**

But we look at our current situation and it appears to be the total opposite.

We know God's word says in **Romans 8:28** that *"all things work together for the good of those that love God and are called according to His purpose"*. We say "that is me!" "I am called and I love God, so this thing must work out for my good." Then we ask, "but why am I here in the desert?" "How can any good come from this?" "What is God's purpose in this trial?"

We know the promises of God. We believe them, we stand on them and even confess and declare them, but nothing has changed. (so it appears) We are more than ready to get out of this trial, this bad situation, and the land of lack. We want to get to the good stuff! We want to get to the fulfillment of the dreams God has shown us for our future. "I am ready for that thriving and growing church or ministry." " I am ready to be the boss and own my own company." "I am ready to get out of debt!" "I am ready to have a wife, or husband and family."

We all have those dreams of the destiny where we just know God wants us to be…but…..I am stuck here in the desert when I want to be in the "promised land" of prosperity, healing and victory.

It reminds me of when we were children and if given the choice, we would eat the cake and ice cream before the vegetables and meat. We would even live on desserts if we were permitted to. We now as adults haven't changed much. We still want the good stuff first!

In the same way or bodies need proper nourishment, and we can not just live on dessert, there is a work that needs to take place in us first before we experience the "dessert" and the Lord knows it.

PS 66:10 *For you, O God, tested us; you refined us like silver.* *PS 66:11* *You brought us into prison and laid burdens on our backs.* *PS 66:12* *You let men ride over our heads; we went through fire and water, but you brought us to a place of abundance.*

We must be tested and refined first! We must go through the fire and water first. Then we will be brought to the place of abundance! He must take us through the desert places at some point in our life if we are to experience the "dessert" or the destiny and all the good stuff we so desire! He must purify us and refine us. You may go through fire and water, but you will be brought to a place of abundance! I have often said the Lord is more concerned about our character then our comfort and that is true.

In this book I will share why "First the Desert, then the Dessert".

I will share personal stories of my own desert experiences and some of what I learned in those desert places. I discovered in God's Word why He takes us through the desert and will share with you how to respond while in the desert and why we sometimes prolong the desert experience.

All of God's Promises are for each and every one of us but there is work He must do in us first! If you are willing to allow the Lord to take you through the desert and learn what you must, you will experience the "dessert"!

You will experience the blessed life that God has for you.
        But first the Desert, then the Dessert!

Chapter 1 – The Promises of God.

Exodus 3:8- *So I have come down to rescue them from the hand of the Egyptians and to <u>bring them up out of that land into a good and spacious land, a land flowing with milk and honey.</u>*

Exodus 3:17- <u>*And I have promised to bring you up out of your misery in Egypt into*</u> *the land of the Canaanites, Hittites, Amorites, Perizzites, Hivites and Jebusites--*<u>*a land flowing with milk and honey.*</u>'

In the Old Testament God promised to bring his children out of Egypt into a good land, a land flowing with milk and honey. They had been in slavery and mistreated for years. God chose Moses to be their leader to bring them out and to bring them into the Promised Land. However they spent 40 years wondering in the "DESERT" and only 'TWO" of the original group got to enjoy the "DESSERT". (the land flowing with milk and honey)

There were many reasons why this happened and I will share some of them in this book.

God has promised many things to us as His children as well. Many Christians today don't experience the DESSERT that He has promised them and they often spend way too much time in the DESERT.

We can experience the DESSERT that God has waiting for us but we will often have to go through the DESERT "FIRST" to get to the DESSERT. I will get into all the details about why the desert first, but I want to encourage you first concerning "The Promises of God."

Joshua 21:45 -*Not one of all the LORD's good promises to the house of Israel failed; every one was fulfilled.*

God's Word is full of good promises for HIS children. Because I am a child of the "Most High God" I have special promises made to me by my Heavenly Father and every one of them will be fulfilled!

This is something we need to know and expect!

2 Corinthians 1:20 *For no matter how many promises God has made, they are "Yes" in Christ. And so through him the "Amen" is spoken by us to the glory of God.*

That verse excites me to know that no matter how many promises God makes they will come to pass in my life!

Psalms 145:13 *The LORD is faithful to all his promises and loving toward all he has made.*

The Lord is faithful to ALL HIS PROMISES! Not just a few of them. But ALL of them! He is faithful to ALL of us, not just some of us. That is a faith builder!

I get excited when I read a verse like **James 1:17** - *"Every good and perfect gift is from above, coming down from the Father of the heavenly lights,..."*

That is good news! EVERY GOOD AND PERFECT GIFT is from our Heavenly Father!

We should live in expectancy that God will send down every good and perfect gift that He has for each and every one of us.

What are some of the good and perfect gifts that God sends down to us?

The first one that comes to mind is obviously **"SALVATION"**!

JN 3:16 "<u>**For God so loved the world that he gave**</u> *his one and only Son, that whoever believes in him shall not perish but have eternal life.* 17 *For God did not send his Son into the world to condemn the world, but to save the world through him.*

<u>**The fact that God sent the best gift of all and that was His Son JESUS to be the sacrifice for my sin!**</u> Jesus paid the price and redeemed me from the curse of the law!

I am now saved, sanctified and heaven bound. There is no greater love and no greater gift then the gift of salvation!

As wonderful as salvation is and although I would not trade it for anything or anyone, there is more!

Some people believe "spiritually" that salvation is all there is. That it ends there. It does not end there and there are more gifts!

There is the promise of the gift of the Holy Spirit
AC 2:38 *Peter replied, "Repent and be baptized, every one of you, in the name of Jesus Christ for the forgiveness of your sins. And <u>**you will receive the gift of the Holy Spirit**</u>.* 39 <u>***The promise is for you and your children and for all who are far off***</u>*--for all whom the Lord our God will call."*

Acts 1:8- *But <u>**you will receive power when the Holy Spirit comes on you**</u>; and you will be my witnesses in Jerusalem, and* *in all Judea and Samaria, and to the ends of the earth."*

The "gift" of the Holy Spirit is an awesome and precious promise available for each and every one of us!

Peace is a wonderful gift and promise from God.
I discovered in the Bible that he desires for us to have real peace!

Jesus said in **John 14:27** *" Peace I leave with you;* <u>*my peace I give you.*</u> *I do not give to you as the world gives…"*

To know that Jesus said He was giving us HIS PEACE is a wonderful thing! To experience that peace that passes all understanding is a good and perfect gift!

People all over the world are searching for peace and we have it!

PS 85:8 *I will listen to what God the LORD will say;* <u>*he promises peace to his people,*</u> *his saints-- but let them not return to folly.*

That verse says that God promises peace to HIS PEOPLE! If you are born again then you are one of His people and you can expect for God to give you peace in every situation and circumstance! Even in the desert, even in your midnight hour you can still have the peace of God!

In the following verses of scripture we have more wonderful promises of God:

In **Psalms 103:2-5** we read: *"Praise the LORD, O my soul, and forget not all his benefits-- PS 103:3 <u>who forgives all your sins and heals all your diseases</u>, PS 103:4 <u>who redeems your life from the pit</u> and <u>crowns you with love and compassion</u>, PS 103:5 <u>who satisfies your desires with good things</u> so that your youth is renewed like the eagle's."*

What powerful reminders of the benefits of serving God! He promises to not only **forgive our sins** but to also **heal our diseases!** **(Psalms 103:3)**

He says in **Exodus 15:26-** .. *"I am the The Lord that heals you"*

I Peter 2:24 - *He himself bore our sins in his body on the tree, so that we might die to sins and live for righteousness<u>; by his wounds you have been healed.</u>*

He promises to **redeem our lives from the pit**! Has anyone reading this been brought out of the pit before?

He goes on to say that He will **crown us with love and compassion**! I will take it!

He will also **satisfy my desires with good things**! I want to be satisfied with good things as well!

Timothy 6:17 in part says to the rich to .. *"put their hope in God, <u>who richly provides us with everything for our enjoyment</u>*

The Lord wants us to enjoy life! Timothy said that God richly provides us with everything for our enjoyment!

These are just a few of the promises we should be familiar with in God's Word and expect to receive from the Lord.

We know that God says that He watches over His Word to perform it!

We find in **Numbers 23:19** that "*God is not a man, that he should lie, nor a son of man, that he should change his mind. Does he speak and then not act?* <u>*Does He promise and not fulfill?*</u>"

We believe and know that what God promises He does fulfill.

If you are sick, <u>**He is your healer.**</u> That is promised all through God's Word. I have experienced divine healing and so has my wife. There have been times "in the desert" though where healing had not yet manifested. But the dessert will come! God has not changed! If you are battling pain and sickness at this moment you can still stand in faith on God's Word and know that Christ is your healer!

<u>**It is God's desire that we prosper and be in health even as our soul prospers**</u>. (3 John 2)

So God desires not only for you to be healthy but to prosper in your soul and financially! Jesus said in **John 10:10** that He came that I may have life and life to the fullest! If I am broke and poor that is NOT God's will for me. Is living life to the fullest being poor? broke? No Way! Lack is not where it's at!

There have been times in my life where I had plenty of money. I was enjoying every bit of it and giving generously where God led me to give. But there have also been times in the desert where money seemed scarce. You need to know if you are in the desert financially that is not the permanent place God has for you. Remain faithful in obeying His Word and at the proper time you will leave the desert and enjoy the dessert!

He will bring you out of the financial desert and to the dessert place of financial prosperity if you will learn and do what you must while in the desert!

We can read in **Deuteronomy 28** all of the blessings that will come upon us and overtake us if we will obey the Lord. There may be times in your life where you are obeying Him, walking in faith and it appears the blessing is hiding from you or that the blessing bank ran out! You may be in the desert place, however it is not a permanent place!

Whatever you may be going through right now or in the future, I want to encourage you to: **hold on, don't quit, don't disobey, don't turn away and God will bring you out of that desert place to that place where the blessings are overflowing in your life**. But remember, "first the desert, then the dessert!

I became a Christian at 21 years of age. I was fortunate enough the past 29 years of serving God to be in churches that preached the "Full Gospel". That Jesus came to save you, heal you, fill you, prosper you and set you free! I praise God for it. But was I rarely ever taught about the desert times or wilderness times in serving God.

We are told in **Psalms 34:19** that *"MANY are the afflictions of the righteous, but the Lord delivers them out of them all"*.

For some reason I don't remember that scripture being preached!

I don't remember a sermon with that verse as a text.

Let the preacher shout, *"Come serve Jesus and have many afflictions!"* I don't think there would be too many people wanting to give their hearts to Jesus on that one!

By the way, the word **"affliction"** actually **means exceedingly great grief, heavy sorrow and trouble.**

There will be the "desert times" of sorrow, trouble, and grief in our lives. But God is with us!

The promise of God is in the rest of the verse that Jesus will deliver you out of them all. It does not mean you won't go through them, but that He will be with you and deliver you.

Even the often quoted **Psalm 23:4** says "Even though I <u>walk through</u> the valley of the shadow of death, I will fear no evil, <u>for you are with me</u>". Praise God I am going through and He is with me!

Shadrach, Meshach and Abednego weren't spared from the fiery furnace, but God was with them and delivered them!

Daniel wasn't spared from the lion's den, but God was with him and he walked out alive!

Paul and Silas were beaten for preaching the gospel and put in prison. They didn't do what most Christians today would do. Whine, gripe and complain. They prayed and sang hymns to God and were delivered!

Yes God has wonderful promises for us all through His Word but nowhere does he promise us a trouble free life!

Jesus told us in **John 16:33**.. *"In this world you will have trouble. But take heart! I have overcome the world."*

Many of us were only taught about the blessing and prosperity side of serving God, and not the fact that even as a Christian we would have trouble.

Because of one-sided teaching, many "believers" have trouble "believing" when trouble comes, when affliction comes, when the desert times come.

They cannot "believe" it is happening to them and then they have trouble believing God for healing, and deliverance.

They often begin to doubt God's love for them and question all that they have believed and been taught. Most have been taught the truth. The problem is that they have been taught only one side of the truth. I am giving you both sides of the truth. The truth is God does desire to bless you, prosper you, heal you and deliver you.

God does desire to give you all things to freely enjoy and every good and perfect gift does come from your Heavenly Father!

But the truth also is that sooner or later trouble will come, desert experiences will come! Your faith will be tested!

But when it does you need to believe and know that God will be with you and will work every situation out for your good as well as be your source of strength!

PS 46:1 *God is our refuge and strength, an ever-present help in trouble.*

PS 18:2 *The LORD is my rock, my fortress and my deliverer; my God is my rock, in whom I take refuge. He is my shield and the horn of my salvation, my stronghold.*

Romans 8:28 *And we know that in all things God works for the good of those who love him, who have been called according to his purpose.*

God's Word is full of many promises for each and every one of us but we need to know all of God's Word not just part of it!

I do not want to "rain on your parade" but I want you to know how to handle trouble when it comes! I want you to be victorious and more than a conqueror! I want you to receive every promise of God!

So you need to know that the TRUTH only sets you free if you know the truth and apply it to your life! Truth unknown or not applied will not help you or set you free! Yes it is true that the Gospel is "Good News"!

The "Good News" is that even though there is trouble in the world, and we will have our share of it, Jesus overcame the world. Since Christ is in us then we too are overcomers and can and will overcome every trial and trouble that comes our way.

As a pastor I would much rather equip you with "ALL" of the truth then just a part of it. You will grow up faster and know that even though there will be afflictions and trouble, that the Lord will deliver you.

When you wake up one day and wonder why you are in the "desert" you will be able to say, "Oh o.k. I know what this is about", and be able to get through it and get to your promised land.

That is why I wrote this book!

The prosperity message is good and is biblical in the proper context. But in it's extremes it can be harmful. Yes God does want you to prosper! Yes God delights in your prosperity! Yes the wealth of the wicked is stored up for you! Yes you are to be blessed to be a blessing! But what are you going to do when you are going through a desert experience where you are not seeing the promised prosperity in your life? Applying what you learn in this book will help you!

Teaching people that if you just live for God and have faith you will never have any trouble and you will live in some supernatural bubble is not true and does more harm then good as well. Yes Faith will accomplish much in your life. We as the just are to live by faith. Yes God does watch over us and protect us, but we live in a sin fallen world where bad people do bad things to good people. We are imperfect people and will make mistakes that can hurt others and us.

What are you going to do if and when a tragedy strikes and you had been taught that nothing bad would happen to you?

I do not believe God kills people, or makes people sick or brings tragedy in your life. BUT....He sometimes allows it!

How are you going to handle it? What will it do to your faith?

Just like a muscle grows when it is stretched and put to use, your faith grows when it is stretched and put to use. When is your faith stretched more then when trouble comes and there is nothing you can do but believe God for your deliverance and breakthrough?

I am a "faith preacher". I am saved by faith and live to please God by my faith and receive everything I do from faith. But my faith has yet to keep me out of the desert! Faith however has kept me while in the desert and seen me through, and it will you as well!

In August of 1983 our first daughter was born premature and died 12 hours after birth. I was only a 1 ½ year old Christian. I was just learning about faith and healing. That was an attack on my faith. It did not make sense.

I am the type that if I believe something then I believe it all the way or no way! If I am going to preach the Word then I must be 100% convinced that it is God's Word and I can count on God to be faithful to His Word! Well I did not understand how this could happen to us.

We were children of God, serving God and growing in our faith. We believed all the promises concerning healing, victory as well as protection. I got alone with God in my pain, with my Bible and told God "I don't understand", "I need answers." Now it would me nice if I could say God spoke and told me exactly why my daughter did not live. But He did not. Instead He took me through the scriptures and showed me several instances where tragedy struck. Times where people living for Him doing more to advance the Kingdom then I was, were killed or died.

For example did you know that the prophet **Elisha suffered and died from an illness**?

2KI 13:14 *Now Elisha was suffering from the illness from which he died.*

Read all the miracles he did by the power of God. Then read how a dead man's body was thrown on Elisha's bones and he was brought back to life. That will make you think.

2KI 13:20 *Elisha died and was buried. Now Moabite raiders used to enter the country every spring. 21 Once while some Israelites were burying a man, suddenly they saw a band of raiders; so **they threw the man's body into Elisha's tomb. When the body touched Elisha's bones, the man came to life and stood up on his feet.***

The Lord reminded me about John the Baptist. He was not only the for-runner of Jesus but was HIS COUSIN. Why did Jesus not intervene when John was put into prison and his head cut off? Did John not have a family? I am sure he was missed and grieved by his family, friends and followers. I am sure Jesus loved his cousin!

MT 14:6 *On Herod's birthday the daughter of Herodias danced for them and pleased Herod so much 7 that he promised with an oath to give her whatever she asked. 8 Prompted by her mother, she said, "Give me here on a platter the head of John the Baptist." 9 The king was distressed, but because of his oaths and* *his dinner guests, he ordered that her request be granted* ^{10} *and had John beheaded in the prison.* ^{11} *His head was brought in on a platter and given to the girl, who carried it to her mother.* ^{12} *John's disciples came and took his body and buried it. Then they went and told Jesus.* MT 14:13 *When Jesus heard what had happened, he withdrew by boat privately to a solitary place. Hearing of this, the crowds followed him on foot from the towns.* ^{14} *When Jesus landed and saw a large crowd, he had compassion on them and healed their sick.*

What did Jesus do when He heard about John's death? He first went to a solitary place. He wanted to be alone. But what happened? Crowds came to Him and out of His compassion He healed their sick!

Well that made no sense to me that He did not 'prevent' John's death. But the Lord was showing me that bad things happen to good people and He does not always prevent it!

I am sharing these to let you know that none of us are exempt and any more special to our Heavenly Father then any other child of God. He loves us all the same and all of God's promises are for each and every one of us.

Although He does not promise us a trouble free live He does promise to be with us, strengthen us, comfort us and see us through!

During this time of seeking the Lord and His Word He then proceeded to share with me some of the other verses I have already shared in this chapter as well as these below:

Matthew 5:4 – *"Blessed are those who mourn, for they will be comforted."*

Psalms 30:5- *weeping may remain for a night, but rejoicing comes in the morning.*

Psalms 46:1- *God is our refuge and strength, an ever-present help in trouble.*

Hebrews 13:5- *.. "Never will I leave you; never will I forsake you."*

Understand that **it rains on the just and the unjust**.
The difference is that we have the Holy Spirit in us to comfort us and strengthen us. We are not alone and God will not forsake us!

Charlotte and I were comforted, our faith grew stronger, and one year later we had another daughter Jenna, who is 26 years old now, married with our first grandson on the way. Two years later we had another daughter, Jillian.

Both of them were miracles and we needed God's intervention during both pregnancies and He came through!

I was in the Military and the doctor that delivered our first daughter was heart broken that we lost her. He told Charlotte that when she got pregnant again that he wanted to see her personally every time. That does not happen in the military. Charlotte did become pregnant but began having the same problem and symptoms as the first one and unless something changed within her body it looked like we could lose this one.

Through a lot of prayer and faith and God's intervention, she was healed and went full term and delivered on her exact due date!

Two years later she became pregnant again. This time we were not in the military and had just moved out of state and for a ministry position. We had no health insurance. We had no clue of how we were going to pay all the doctors and hospital bills but God came through THE WEEK she delivered and all but about $200.00 was covered.

If the financial concern was not enough Charlotte got blood clots in her legs and was told to be on bed rest. (which she ignored) She was in a lot of pain and anytime she woke up in the middle of the night her leg would be numb. Blood clots can kill. So here I am looking at it that this time Satan isn't trying to just take my daughter but now he wants my wife! We prayed. I fasted. Then God totally healed her leg and all blood clots disappeared and all pain left. That is the short story. The healing did not come over night. She was in pain for several weeks. But we stood on the PROMISES of God and He delivered!

My prayer through this chapter and this book is that your faith be increased in the promises of God and in His faithfulness. That you do receive every gift and every promise that He has for you.

Part of that increased faith is to know that God knows what He is doing in your life and during those desert experiences where it appears all hope is lost and you are confused and nothing makes sense. I want you to remember what you have read here and KNOW that GOD IS FAITHFUL!

During this chapter I have shared just some of the promises in God's Word. There are many more and I encourage you to get all of them into your spirit.

Memorize them, pray and confess them, but know that doing those things will not keep you from **some of the God designed desert experiences He has for you.**

There are times where the enemy comes and attacks. Every attack from the enemy is an attack on our faith. The question is are you going to keep your faith?

Jesus asked if he would find faith on the earth when He returned.

Luke 18:8-… when the Son of Man comes, will he find faith on the earth?"

At the end of his life, Paul said in **11 Timothy 4:7** – "I have fought the good fight, I have finished the race, I have kept the faith. 8 Now there is in store for me the crown of righteousness, which the Lord, the righteous Judge, will award to me on that day--and not only to me, but also to all who have longed for his appearing.

Read through the scriptures and see what all Paul went through for the cause of Christ. Yet at the end of his life he was able to say he had kept his faith AND that there was an award waiting for him as well as those of us who keep our faith as well!

Life itself could be compared to a desert but then in eternal life we receive the dessert!

The point is there is an enemy and his name is Satan. He comes to try and steal from you, kill you and destroy you. There are circumstances in your life that are the direct result of that.

But there are also times when God places you in the desert!

That is more of what I am addressing in this book.

In our case I am not saying it was God's plan that our first daughter died. I do not believe that for one minute. The thief 'Satan" comes to steal kill and destroy. But during that desert time for us, God used it as a time for us to grow and to learn to trust Him even more. He turned a bad situation around and used it to make us stronger and we have been able to minister to others who have gone through a similar situation.

Satan can't and will not ever defeat you unless you let him! You need to know that God is a good God!

Even though He may not protect you **from** every trouble, trial and tragedy, His ultimate plan for your life can't be stopped! (unless you give up and quit) Every promise in God's Word is for you and for me!

There will be dessert but you will probably go through the desert first!

In the next chapter I will begin to explain what is the "desert"? and why the desert?

Why do we go through some of the desert experiences we do and who is responsible for it?

Chapter 2- Why The Desert?

Before I get into the meat of this chapter on "Why the Desert" I need to explain what exactly is the desert.

The desert is deserted place.
A place of the unknown.
A place with scarcity of water.
A place with extremes. Extreme heat, extreme winds and extreme thirst. Extreme loneliness.
Many people have died in the desert due to lack of nourishment.

When you are going through a desert experience, you often feel deserted. It feels like God has left you to fend for yourself. You often do not sense His presence although He is really there.

You don't know what is going on in your life.

You may experience a spiritual dryness and you are thirsty for the things of God as well as a touch from God.

There are often extremes in your circumstances. You may be going through extreme financial difficulties, as well as other troubles and trials.

You often feel that if God doesn't come through for you and provide in some miraculous way that you won't survive.

In the same way a desert experience can be a place of "death". By that I mean death to your flesh. Death to your will, your plans, and desires.

The desert brings you to a place of total dependency on the Lord because you have no control over your life and unless God comes through there is no way out!

This my friend is what I mean when I am talking about a desert experience. You are in between where you once were and the place you really want to be, and it is not a pleasurable place to be.

The inspiration from this book came in part by a message the Lord gave me to preach to my congregation as well as minister to myself while I was in a desert experience.

The text came from the following verses:

DT 8:1 *Be careful to follow every command I am giving you today, so that you may live and increase and may enter and possess the land that the LORD promised on oath to your forefathers. 2 Remember how the LORD your God led you all the way in the desert these forty years, to humble you and to test you in order to know what was in your heart, whether or not you would keep his commands. 3 He humbled you, causing you to hunger and then feeding you with manna, which neither you nor your fathers had known, to teach you that man does not live on bread alone but on every word that comes from the mouth of the LORD.*

If I were there in person and were to ask each of you reading these verses, most notably verse one, if you want to LIVE AND INCREASE and ENTER AND POSSESS THE LAND the Lord has promised you. I imagine all of you would say yes! Of course!

Anyone that could read could determine that if I want to live and increase and enter and possess the promises of God then I need to be careful to follow every command God has given me. That would be the right answer!

The bible also speaks of the willing and obedient eating the good of the land. **(Isaiah 1:19)**

To obey is better than sacrifice. **(I Samuel 15:22)**

Joshua 1:8 is one of my favorite verses of scripture and states: *"Do not let this Book of the Law depart from your mouth; meditate on it day and night, so that you may be careful to do everything written in it. Then you will be prosperous and successful".*

What a promise! If I meditate in God's Word and obey it then I will be prosperous and successful! I love it!

You don't need to pay large sums of money to some wealthy sinner at a seminar to tell you how to prosper and be successful! Just follow the principles in God's Word!

This is one of the main promises in God's Word and will not fail! Now some may claim that I am using Old Testament scriptures and we are no longer under the law but under the better covenant of "grace". I will not argue that. But the fact is we are still to obey God and obedience to God brings His blessing! He does not reward disobedience!

1JN 2:3 <u>We know that we have come to know him if we obey his commands.</u> ⁴ <u>The man who says, "I know him," but does</u>

not do what he commands is a liar, and the truth is not in him. ⁵ *But if anyone obeys his word, God's love is truly made complete in him. This is how we know we are in him:* ⁶ *Whoever claims to live in him must walk as Jesus did.*

According to 1 John 2:3 if we don't obey His commands then we don't even know God! It goes as far as to call you a liar!

The Bible tells us faith works by love. This verse tells us that God's love is made complete in us if we obey him! So your faith will only work if God's love is complete in you and that will only happen if you obey His Word!

1JN 3:21 Dear friends, if our hearts do not condemn us, we have confidence before God ²² *and **receive from him anything we ask, because we obey his commands and do what pleases him**.*

Do you want your prayers answered for healing, blessing, prosperity, promotion etc? Then your prayers will only work if you obey His commands and do what pleases Him!

So God's principals are still the same! You want to live and increase? You want to enter into your promised land?
Then you must obey God's Word and live a life that is pleasing to Him! The difference now is you do it by faith knowing He is with and in you to help you!

But what does all of this have to do with "First the Desert then the Dessert"? Or the title of this chapter, "Why the Desert?"

Back to our text. Deuteronomy Chapter 8 started with the

instruction in verse one to obey God so that you may live and increase.

It all begins with obedience! But then it goes on in verse: *² Remember how the LORD your God led you all the way in the desert these forty years, to humble you and to test you in order to know what was in your heart, whether or not you would keep his commands. ³ He humbled you, causing you to hunger and then feeding you with manna, which neither you nor your fathers had known, to teach you that man does not live on bread alone but on every word that comes from the mouth of the LORD.*

These two verses are the main points of this book and teaching.

In beginning to understand "why the desert" you need to understand who led you there.

Deut 8:2 *Remember how* **the LORD your God led you all the way in the desert….**

I need to repeat that verse again: ***Deut 8:2*** *Remember how* **the LORD your God led you all the way in the desert….**

What?? You mean the LORD led me into this desert? Are you kidding? Are you crazy?

The WORD says "every good and perfect gift comes from God." This is far from good and perfect!

The WORD says "JESUS came that I may live life to the fullest!" THIS is not living life to the fullest!

This is where many of us get tripped up. We find ourselves in the desert and we think the devil put us there because it is the opposite of all the promises of God. We spend our time "binding" and "rebuking" the devil and nothing changes. Then we get frustrated and confused.

Now there are times where you may find yourself in an apparent "desert" and it is just the result of sin or bad choices you have made. The devil is not to blame and the Lord did not lead you there. That is when you need to be quick to repent, ask for forgiveness and for God's mercy.

In this book though, I am talking about the desert experience that GOD DOES LEAD YOU TO although these principals can help either way.

One way you will know the Lord has brought you there is when you have searched your heart and there is nothing in particular that you have done to end up there. You know you are obeying God and doing your best to live a life that is pleasing to Him. That is when you need to realize that the Lord has placed you there and it is for a reason.

The times it may just be the devil is when he tempted you with sin and you gave in and now you are "reaping what you have sown". Satan tempts, God tests. There is a difference.

When God has led you to the desert is not the time to begin whining, gripping or complaining. All of the binding and rebuking and confessing the Word will not change anything. Open your heart and mind to hear what the Lord wants to do in your life and seek His face to what "Dessert" He is preparing you for! This is a time where you should get excited because you know the Lord is preparing you for something great!

JAMES 1:2 *Consider it pure joy, my brothers, whenever you face trials of many kinds*, *3 because you know that the testing of your faith develops perseverance. 4 Perseverance must finish its work so that you may be mature and complete, not lacking anything.*

Notice the above verse says WHENEVER you face trials of MANY kinds. Again you will face trials and it probably will not just be a few. James goes on to speak concerning the "testing of our faith". That is God's doing so there is no use trying to fight God!

God is more concerned about your spiritual growth and maturity then you "feeling good". God is more concerned about your character then your being comfortable!

I consider being in the desert a time when I am facing trials of many kinds. Now there are few ways that I can respond.

I can respond the biblical way and that is with JOY or I can respond the way many others have including the children of Israel and prolong my stay. I personally want out of the desert as soon as possible! So I choose Joy!

Getting back to our scriptures in Deuteronomy. I can just hear some of you saying again "Well now that was Old Testament and that was just one instance where God led people into the desert."

LUKE 4:1 *Jesus, full of the Holy Spirit, returned from the Jordan and <u>was led by the Spirit in the desert</u>, ² where for forty days he was tempted by the devil.* He ate nothing during those days, and at the end of them he was hungry.

What? JESUS – FULL OF THE HOLY SPIRIT was LED BY THE SPIRIT in the desert where He was tempted by the devil?

See this is where we get all messed up! We think because I am BORN AGAIN and SPIRIT FILLED that I am exempt from trials, tests and or temptations. If we aren't thinking that, then again we are blaming the devil for our journey to the desert.

If JESUS was led by the Spirit to the desert what makes you think you are exempt? There was a purpose for Jesus being LED BY THE SPIRIT into the desert and there is for you as well!

This is where I am so glad the Lord has placed a heavy emphasis on me to be a "teacher" as well as preacher. I can effectively teach and equip people in "sound doctrine" and if they will listen and apply what I teach they will grow up and thereby save themselves from a lot of future frustration!

If it was necessary for JESUS to be led into the desert to be tempted by the devil how much more is it for you and I? The best part is when Jesus passed the test He returned in the power of the Spirit and His ministry really took off!

In closing this chapter you need to realize in "Why the Desert?" that it is often the Lord that is sending you there and if the Lord is sending you there, it is for a good reason. **There are also times that although I do not believe God sends you there.**

He has allowed it. Times where maybe you did lose a child. Times where you are fighting sickness and pain and the healing has not manifested. These can be considered desert experiences so you may as well as learn and grow.

Now hear me I am NOT saying God puts sickness on you or kills someone you love to teach you something. That would be a cruel and unjust God. I would not even think of breaking my daughter's arm to teach her a lesson. I don't believe God kills people or makes you sick to humble you or test you either. However there may be times whether it be from an attack from Satan, or bad judgment on our part where death or sickness comes and we feel like we are in the desert. You are there, God allowed it so you may as well get something out of it!

Your attitude and acceptance of the fact that at this time this is the Lord's will for you, or **that He did allow this to take place in your life** will do much in you learning all that you need to learn as well as grow leaps in bound in your faith walk. It will also do much in you accepting the fact that God is preparing you for a greater work and wanting to help you grow up and mature spiritually!

Deut 8:2 *Remember how the LORD your God led you all the way in the desert these forty years**, to humble you and to test you** in order to know what was in your heart, whether or not you would keep his commands.* ³ **He humbled you**, *causing you to hunger and then feeding you with manna, which neither you nor your fathers had known**, to teach you** that man does not live on bread alone but on every word that comes from the mouth of the LORD.*

In closing this chapter in answering Why the desert? In the above text there are three reasons why God takes us through the desert.

They are:

1. To Humble You
2. To Test You
3. To Teach You

The next few chapters I will go into detail on why we need to be humbled, tested and taught!

Chapter 3- Humility Before Honor

PR 15:33 *The fear of the LORD teaches a man wisdom, and humility comes before honor.*

PR 18:12 *Before his downfall a man's heart is proud, but humility comes before honor.*

Why the desert before the dessert? Why humility before honor?

Because it is apart of our sinful nature to be proud! Just because we become a child of God at the new birth does not mean every part of the old nature is gone! Yes our spirit is alive unto God, but WE have to put our old man down and pride is one of the last things we want to see die. Our old father the devil was full of pride and that was the cause of his downfall.

ISA 14:12 *How you have fallen from heaven, O morning star, son of the dawn! You have been cast down to the earth, you who once laid low the nations!* **ISA 14:13** *You said in your heart, "**I will** ascend to heaven; **I will** raise my throne above the stars of God; I will sit enthroned on the mount of assembly, on the utmost heights of the sacred mountain.* **ISA 14:14** ***I will*** *ascend above the tops of the clouds; I will make myself like the Most High."* **ISA 14:15** *But you are brought down to the grave, to the depths of the pit.*

Lucifer was full of pride with all of his " I wills". Many of us begin the same way and for the Lord to be able to use us and trust us that pride must be rooted out!

If we do not come to a place of true humility and the Lord were to give us every gift He has for us, we would be just like Lucifer in declaring all that we were and all that we were going to do and where is God in any of that?

If the Lord were to give us the ultimate ministry or career He has for us when we were still walking in pride then we would be so full of ourselves and in thinking it was all about us and that we did it! Then HE would have to bring us down!

PR 16:18 *Pride goes before destruction, a haughty spirit before a fall.*

Do you want to start all over? I don't! If God gave us the dessert before the desert we would be so full of self it would be pathetic! We would feel we have no need for God. "Look what I did!" Look what I accomplished" We would think that we were the one on the throne, we would be in control of our lives, and THAT is not God's plan for any of us.

Before God can bring us to a place of honor, before God can bring about the fulfillment of our ministry or careers we must be humbled! He takes us through the desert to bring us to that place of humility. The place where we have no control over the situations and circumstances in our lives. A place where we can't plot and plan our way out. A place where we come to realize that without God I am nothing and can do nothing! A place of total trust and dependency on the Lord. A place where we will not take any credit but where it will be all about us saying "Look what the Lord has done"!

In our text in Deut 8: **2** *Remember how the LORD your God led you all the way in the desert these forty years<u>, to humble you</u> and to test you in order to know what was in your heart, whether or not you would keep his commands.* **3** <u>*He humbled you, causing you to hunger and then feeding you with manna*</u>……..

Who led you in the desert? We already discussed it, but God did! Why? **TO HUMBLE YOU!** (in verse 2 and 3)

Verse 3 says He humbled you causing you to hunger and THEN FEEDING YOU WITH MANNA!

That is where I got the "dessert"! He led them into the desert then after they were humbled and hungry He fed them "manna".

EX 16:31 *The people of Israel called the bread manna.* <u>*It was white like coriander seed and tasted like wafers made with honey.*</u>

Manna is described as a bread that tasted like wafers made with honey. To me that is something sweet and comparable to a type of dessert.

The first purpose in God leading you into the desert is to bring you to a place of total humility and a place of total hunger and dependency on the Lord.

He is a jealous God. He does not want us having a hunger and passion for all of the worldly things we often do. Because we are often just as stubborn as the Israelites were, this is the only way He can really get our attention. We may think we are going about our Father's business and walking in humility but often we are not. If we aren't "hearing" or learning in other ways then He will take us to the desert!

I need to repeat something again so I am not misunderstood. God does not put sickness on you to humble you. That is not how God operates! He cannot be a healer and killer all in one!

He said, "I am the God that heals you"- not the God that makes you sick! God will not kill your loved ones to get pride out of you either. Again, there is one that kills and his name is Satan. God gives life, Satan takes life.

If you are fighting sickness and disease and while seeking the Lord and believing for healing and He reveals pride or any sin in your life. Yes by all means deal with it! Those things can be a hindrance to your healing. But God did not put sickness on you to humble you or teach you.

Now I want to share from a personal example in my life of a desert experience. In part I was to blame but I also know that the Lord took me there for this and other purposes. Several years ago I had a period of time where I was not in any kind of pastoral ministry. I ended up getting into an awesome secular business where I went from a previous job making $20,000 a year to $60,000 in one year. Then went on to earn around $100,000 a year for the next 3 years.

In the middle of this I got back involved in ministry and pioneered our church with one other family. I was enjoying the "blessed" life! We bought our dream home, dream cars, went on dream vacations and life was great! On top of that I began pastoring and fulfilling what I knew was the true "call" on my life.

Because of the money I was making and the tithes we gave to the church we were able to rent two storefront buildings side by side with about 15 people in the church. Why? Because the tithes my wife and I gave could cover the rent whether anyone else tithed or not. Well the church began to grow, "slowly" and the giving from everyone else grew as well. So I am thinking this is great! The church will keep growing and over time I can do less and less of the business and eventually be a full-time pastor but still rake the money in from owning the business.

How many of you realize that often the Lord's plans and our plans are not on the same page?

Well to make a long story short- in less than a year I lost my business! I lost 100k a year of income! We lost our house and a car. I had also sold my dream car prior to losing the other one. We also had to sell off the investment properties we had. If that all was not bad enough, we also lost half the people in our church all in the same few months of the same year.

We were in financial ruin! There was nothing else "I" could do to make that kind of money and pay on all the debts I had acquired! Now I know that God is our source and that He is the God of the breakthrough and could provide all of our needs etc. We stood in faith, believing God would come through. We gave to other ministries expecting our financial harvest to come through and "save" the day! Well in our case there was no harvest and no financial breakthrough.

He let the bottom all fall out and we were in the desert.

To say I was humbled and humiliated is an understatement!

I do need to say here and now that none of this has changed our faith in the Lord in anyway concerning prosperity and Him meeting our needs or being a miracle working God!

Now it was not about the "stuff". We are not materialistic people even though we believe in biblical prosperity and were enjoying the things that money can buy and loved being able to give to others.

We know we are not to chase money and wealth, or trust in uncertain riches. But we also know the Lord delights in our prosperity and blesses us financially so that we can be used by Him to in turn be a blessing to others.

For those that may question our lifestyle before losing it all, I will quote a statement I heard someone say and that is "Don't judge my harvest when you don't know my seed". Our giving back then ended up being equal to my wife's annual salary and she worked a full time job! We gave to missions and anywhere and anytime the Lord led us to. We have always been faithful tithers and givers!

The problem was I did not do it all God's way and He knew there was pride in me that needed to be removed if I was to go to the Promised Land. (the ultimate in "Ministry" that He has for me). He also knew that even though I said I would if He told me to, I would not just walk away from the business that I loved and the money it brought in. Certainly not with the small congregation I had and with what income the church was bringing in.

During this time the Lord would also not let me go start another business or seek full time employment outside of our church!

I also need to say again that in the middle of this, the growth we experienced in the church we lost in a matter of a few months. So not only was my business and income from that gone, but ½ my church was gone! We had to give up one of the storefront buildings and have children, youth and adults all in one small building.

Now at the time prior to all of this I did not believe there was any pride in me. But while in the desert I began hearing from the Lord loud and clear! Part of what I heard was that all of those years I thought I was trusting "God" for our finances I wasn't! I was trusting in my business and the work of my hands! I had no problem getting into debt and borrowing any amount of money I wanted for what I wanted because I knew that there was plenty of money coming in from "my" business that I could pay on all of it!

The problem was my faith and trust was in the wrong place. (not to mention the debt issue) The Lord revealed to me even in us renting the storefronts there was no faith in Him. After all I could pay the rent from my business whether we had anyone in the church giving or not! He showed me how I wanted all the control in everything! Wanting to be in control is a "pride" issue! Guess what the Lord does with pride?

Believe me when you go through what we did- you have no control and pride becomes a thing of the past. Here I was 44 years old and pastoring a small church (actually starting it over again) with very little income and starting all over financially.

PR 11:2 *When pride comes, then comes disgrace, but with humility comes wisdom.*

I felt disgraced! But humility came, and along with it WISDOM!

It is amazing what wisdom will do for you!

THIS time it will all be done the right way!

THIS time I am trusting in GOD to meet our needs!

THIS time it is ALL about HIS WILL and not mine!

We will have financial prosperity again but God's way!

PR 22:4 *Humility and the fear of the LORD bring wealth and honor and life.*

If you want God's wealth, God's honor and God's way of Life then get humility!

So here I was in the desert- humbled and disgraced, but gaining wisdom and...... God was moving in our lives and in our church in ways I would have never imagined and never experienced if we had stayed on the same path we were before.

He had brought us to the desert but we were looking forward to the dessert for we know the Promised Land is just ahead!

In my case God has called me to be an apostle and there is no higher calling. For me to be the kind of apostle He needs me to be then there is no place for pride! In no part of my life or ministry can I be permitted to be in control or on the throne!

Even if I were not in the preaching ministry there would still be no room for pride! As an ambassador for Christ there can be no pride in me and the same goes for you!

As a Christian we all are to be witnesses for Christ! Pride has no in any of us!
I want to remind you of another man that God called and was used tremendously in building the New Testament church. This man however was full of pride and God had to knock him off of his high horse.

That man's name was Saul!

In **Acts Chapter 8** Stephen was stoned to death and Saul stood by and watched. He not only watched but also gave approval to his death. Saul then began to persecute the church and even dragged believers from their houses and had them put into prison. Saul was a very educated man and "religious" man. But a man full of pride and a persecutor of the church. God had other plans for his life!

AC 9:1 Meanwhile, Saul was still breathing out murderous threats against the Lord's disciples. He went to the high priest 2 and asked him for letters to the synagogues in Damascus, so that if he found any there who belonged to the Way, whether men or women, he might take them as prisoners to Jerusalem. <u>3 As he neared Damascus on his journey, suddenly a light from heaven flashed around him. 4 He fell to the ground and heard a voice say to him, "Saul, Saul, why do you persecute me?" AC 9:5 "Who are you, Lord?" Saul asked. "I am Jesus, whom you are persecuting," he replied. 6 "Now get up and go into the city, and you will be told what you must do."</u> AC 9:7 The men traveling with Saul stood there speechless; they heard the sound but did not see anyone. *8 Saul got up from the ground, but when he opened his eyes he could see nothing. So they led him by the hand into Damascus. 9 For three days he was blind, and did not eat or drink anything.*

In verses 3-5 we see where the Lord got Saul's attention and "knocked him off of his high horse"!

Meanwhile the Lord was speaking to Ananias in a vision and had this to say concerning Saul:

AC 9:15 *But the Lord said to Ananias, "Go! **This man is my chosen instrument** to carry my name before the Gentiles and their kings and before the people of Israel. 16 I will show him how much he must suffer for my name."*

Saul's name was changed and he became Paul. Any of you that know your bible, know how much Paul's life was changed as well. You read all that he went through and all that He did as God's chosen instrument in building the kingdom of God.

Acts 20:19- *I served the Lord **with great humility** and with tears, although **I was severely tested** by the plots of the Jews*

Paul learned humility even as he states here that he served the Lord with "great humility". He also refers to being severely tested. I will be sharing concerning that in the next chapter!

2CO 12:7 *To keep me from becoming conceited because of these surpassingly great revelations, there was given me a thorn in my flesh, a messenger of Satan, to torment me. 8 Three times I pleaded with the Lord to take it away from me. 9 But he said to* me, "My grace is sufficient for you, for my power is made perfect in weakness." Therefore I will boast all the more gladly about my weaknesses, so that Christ's power may rest on me.

Paul was used mightily of God and received great revelations from the Lord. Paul states it here and this shows again how much so the Lord is against pride and conceit. Paul was given what he calls a "thorn in the flesh" to **keep him from becoming conceited**. Now some people try to say that it was sickness or blindness. That is NOT what it was. Paul tells us exactly what the thorn in the flesh was. It was a "messenger of Satan". What is a messenger of Satan? Most likely a demon! What is a messenger of God? An Angel!

Paul says he pleaded three times with the Lord to take it away from him. The Lord did not. The Lord wanted Paul totally dependent upon the Lord and HIS power and with no pride!

Everywhere Paul went he was persecuted and harassed. He tells of his shipwreck, stonings, being left for dead. I would say the devil was constantly harassing, buffeting and tormenting him everywhere he went. I would say Paul spent more time in the desert then anywhere else. But his only concern was fulfilling the destiny that God had for him no matter what the cost! Can you say the same thing about your life?

Acts 20:23-24 *I only know that in every city the Holy Spirit warns me that prison and hardships are facing me.* 24 However, *I consider my life worth nothing to me,* if only I may finish the race and complete the task the Lord Jesus has given me--the task of testifying to the gospel of God's grace.

Look at this! The Holy Spirit warned Paul that in EVERY CITY he went to prison and hardships were facing him. Can any of us say our trials, trouble or afflictions compare to that? But look at Paul's heart: He considered his life worth nothing! His only concern was finishing the task the Lord had given him. The task of testifying to the gospel of God's grace.

That kind of puts my cares and concerns to shame. Makes me look at my heart and my motives. I pray it does the same for you.

We can learn an a lot from Paul's life as well as many others in the scriptures. The Lord's desire is that every one of us as His children walks in humility!

The Lord may not call you to be an apostle or to pastor a church, but He has called you to be an ambassador for Christ. He has called you to BE a witness. He has called you to do your part in building His kingdom. You need to know that no man or woman with pride can be used to his or her full potential. God WILL take you to the desert and will keep you there to humble you if necessary. You may believe as I did that you are not a prideful person. But God knows your heart. If you find yourself in the desert one day then there just may some pride in you that needs to go!

Learn from my experience, learn from Paul's as well as the other examples in the scriptures.

If you are going through a desert experience or do in the future, Let God do in you what He must, knowing that HUMILITY COMES BEFORE HONOR and that the desert comes before the dessert! Is it painful? Yes! Will you want to be somewhere else? Yes! But when the Lord is through with molding you into who HE wants you to be it will be worth it all!

Chapter 4 - To Be Tested

Deut 8:2 . *Remember how the LORD your God led you all the way in the desert these forty years, to humble you **and to test you in order to know what was in your heart, whether or not you would keep his commands.***

The second purpose or reason that you may find yourself in the desert when you would rather be enjoying the dessert, is that God needs to TEST you!

Why in the world does God need to TEST me?

"in order to know what was in your heart"

God always has been and always will be concerned with our hearts! He is concerned with what is in our hearts! In order for Him to know what is in our hearts we must be tested!

It is a biblical fact that God tests the heart.

1 Chron 29:17- *I know, my God, that **you test the heart** and are pleased with integrity.*

Proverbs 21:2 *All a man's ways seem right to him, but **the LORD weighs the heart.***
We may think we are ready for the promotion.

We may think that we are ready to pastor that big church.

We may think we are ready to go on the evangelistic field.

We may think we are ready to lead the worship, or lead the youth ministry.

We may think we are ready to be a wife, or husband or parent.
We may think we are ready to be a business owner or real estate guru.

But....

The Lord looks at the heart!

When the Lord had Samuel choose a king he gave him the criteria God looks for:

1SA 16:7 *But the LORD said to Samuel, "Do not consider his appearance or his height, for I have rejected him. The LORD does not look at the things man looks at. Man looks at the outward appearance, but the LORD looks at the heart."*

Man may look at your appearance.
Man may look at your education or talents.
Man may look at your resume and your accomplishments.
Man may look at your past.

But God looks at the heart and God will test your heart!

The question is when He does will you pass the test?

PS 17:3 *Though you probe my heart and examine me at night, though you test me, you will find nothing; I have resolved that my mouth will not sin.*

Can you say as David did, that though God PROBES your heart, examines you at night and TESTS you that He will find nothing? Nothing means anything that does not belong! Those things that cause you to SIN? Or how about our old enemy PRIDE or wrong motives?

When you are tested, when God probes your heart what will He find? You may say as David, "nothing" but when you are taken to the desert to be tested the Lord will see!

In the desert there will be extreme pressure applied and what is in you will come out!

Before the Lord will promote you in ministry, secular career or trust you with financial wealth He has to know what is in your heart.

Are your motives right?

Can He trust you to do what is ethical and moral at all times?
Will you instead deny your integrity at the drop of a hat?
Will you walk in pride and arrogance?
These are all areas of character that must be tested.

Being tested and in the desert will bring out either the best or worst in a person.

The Israelites kept going around in circles for 40 years because the wrong thing kept coming out of their hearts.

How long will you stay in the desert? Much of that depends on what's in your heart and what comes out when you are tested!

Luke 6:45 *The good man brings good things out of the good stored up in his heart, and the evil man brings evil things out of the evil stored up in his heart. For out of the overflow of his heart his mouth speaks.*
According to the above scripture what is stored in your heart is either good or bad and what is stored in your heart comes out!

How does God know whether it is good or bad stored in your heart? That is easy! By what comes out of your mouth!

The Word says in the last line of Luke 6:45- *"For out of the overflow of his heart his mouth speaks"*.

The Lord can tell and others can tell what is in your heart by what comes out of your mouth during a time of trouble, trial and tribulation!

That is the main way you pass or fail the test. If when trouble comes you whine, gripe, complain, lash out at God or others then guess what? You failed!

If everything coming out of your mouth is negative then you failed the test. Have you ever said anything like "I just knew this would happen to me"? " I knew God wouldn't come through for me" "Everybody else gets a blessing but me" "This is just my luck" If that is your response then: YOU FAILED! YOU FAILED! YOU FAILED!

I can just see some of you tuning me out now thinking I am being too harsh. I said earlier the truth would set you free. So if this is how you respond when pressure comes, or trouble comes then you need this truth and to apply it to your life!

I want people to get free from applying what is in this book. I want us all in as few desert experiences as we have to and to get out of them and into feasting on the dessert as soon as possible!

Stop the negative, garbage talking out of your mouth! In order to do that you have to get the garbage out of your heart first!

All the Israelites did was gripe and complain and keep going back into sin and they suffered for it! For entertainments sake let's read some of their foolish complaining. Remember, *"out of the overflow of the heart the mouth speaks"*

NU 11:1 *Now **the people complained about their hardships in the hearing of the LORD**, and when he heard them his anger was aroused.*

That tells me the Lord is not pleased or impressed with complaining!

Exodus 14:11 *They said to Moses, **"Was it because there were no graves in Egypt that you brought us to the desert to die?** What have you done to us by bringing us out of Egypt?* ¹² *Didn't we say to you in Egypt, `Leave us alone; let us serve the Egyptians'? **It would have been better for us to serve the Egyptians than to die in the desert!"***

Some Christians have said the same thing in saying they were better off before they became a Christian. Because of the attacks of the enemy, or the testing of the Lord they get uncomfortable and feel they would be better off back in the world! (Egypt)

Exodus 16:2 *In the desert the **whole community grumbled against Moses and Aaron**.* ³ *The Israelites said to them, "If only we had died by the LORD's hand in Egypt! There we sat around pots of meat and ate all the food we wanted, but **you have brought us out into this desert to starve this entire assembly to death**."*

The WHOLE COMMUNITY grumbled! They went as far as to say they would have been better off to die in Egypt! What foolishness!

But how many of us have ever said the same type of things? Moses was their pastor. I would surely not want a congregation like them!

NU 21:4 *They traveled from Mount Hor along the route to the Red Sea, to go around Edom. But **the people grew impatient on the way; 5 they spoke against God and against Moses, and said, "Why have you brought us up out of Egypt to die in the desert? There is no bread! There is no water! And we detest this miserable food!"***

This time they spoke against GOD AND MOSES. Complain, complain, complain. If you know the story only TWO people out of the original group left the desert and entered into the Promised Land. All of the rest failed their tests and died in the desert!

Many Christians today are no different, and because they keep failing their tests they keep staying in the desert and some will go to their grave never experiencing all that God had promised them.

If you notice it says that they grew "impatient" on the way.
WE never grow "impatient" do we? Ha!
That is another heart issue that the Lord looks at.
If you have a problem with "patience" than you can be pretty sure it will be dealt with by the Lord! This is one of my hot buttons! I have, through much trial, trouble and tribulation over

the years grown to be a lot more patient then I used to be. I just wish the Lord would hurry up and fill my church, fix the people that need fixed, get me all the money I need and do everything else I have been waiting on! (THIS IS A JOKE FATHER!)

COL 3:12 *Therefore, as God's chosen people, holy and dearly loved,* <u>***clothe yourselves with***</u> *compassion, kindness, humility, gentleness and* <u>*patience.*</u>

Are you clothed with compassion? It will come out when tested if you are. Are you clothed with kindness and gentleness? Again, the Lord will see if that is what is really in your heart! Our good friend "Humility" is there and lest you get impatient with me- patience!

James 1:4 *Perseverance must finish its work so that you may be mature and complete, not lacking anything*

As I said earlier He is more concerned about your character than your comfort! Perseverance (patience) must finish its work because God wants you to come to that place of maturity!

In so many positions and places in life patience will so much so be required of you. If it is lacking then you will not succeed in all that God desires for you. So get patience and get it now! lol

As much as you may be in a hurry to get through the dessert and onto bigger and better things, watch out that you aren't too impatient!

Back to the heart and mouth parallel. Proverbs 17:3 ...*I have resolved that my mouth will not sin.*

Have you resolved that your mouth will not sin? God will see when you are tested because the following verse says this:

PR 15:28 *The heart of the righteous weighs its answers, but the mouth of the wicked gushes evil.*

I can not emphasize it enough of the heart and mouth connection. If your heart is right when tested, you will think twice before you speak. If your heart is not where it needs to be you can't help but gush out evil!

I have known people over the years that their life never changes. They go from one bad situation to another. They never grow and mature in the Lord and all they do is gush out a bunch of garbage from their mouth- revealing what is in their heart and why they are where they are!

PR 4:23 <u>*Above all else, guard your heart, for it is the wellspring of life.*</u> **PR 4:24** *Put away perversity from your mouth; keep corrupt talk far from your lips.*

We are told to GUARD our HEART for **it is the wellspring of life**. The type of life that we have is dependent on what is in our heart!

That is one reason why the Lord is so concerned with what is in our heart. What is in our heart will determine what kind of person we will be and if we are ready for the "dessert"!

MT 15:*18 But the things that come out of the mouth come from the heart, and these make a man `unclean.' 19 For out of the heart come evil thoughts, murder, adultery, sexual immorality,* *theft, false testimony, slander.*

Jesus was instructing the disciples and Pharisees because they were concerned about "hand washing" and other traditions of men. Jesus said that the outward isn't what really matters but what is in the heart.

Let's see what Jesus said can come out of the heart:

Evil Thoughts! Murder! Adultery! Sexual Immorality! Theft! False Testimony! Slander!

Now these are just examples that Jesus used. But think about these. If any of those things are in your heart, are you the type of person God is going to want to bless and promote?

Especially someone wanting to be "in the preaching ministry" or in service in the church.

Would God wan to put someone with adultery in his or her heart at the head of a church?

Would God want a young man with "lust" in his heart to be a "youth pastor"?

Would God put someone with "greed" or "theft" in his or her heart over the church treasury! (I could preach here concerning 'theft' and "tithes" but I won't!)

Well I will say this: If you are robbing God in tithes and offerings you are not passing any test and will not be seeing the dessert any time soon! You will have an extended stay at the Desert Inn!

You need to understand that the Lord is smarter than that.

He wants to see what is in your heart BEFORE He promotes you to Pastor, or Worship Leader or Business Owner…or… you fill in the blank!

While you are in the desert this is probably one of the most intense and miserable times of your life. If you can under those conditions stand strong and good things come out of your mouth because your heart is pure, then you will pass the test!

During our desert time when I lost my business, income, home, car etc. the Lord and our church saw what was in my and my wife's heart. We continued to Praise God in the midst of adversity. We allowed Him to reveal any areas of pride. We searched our hearts and repented of anything He revealed to us. I won't say we "never" complained, but when we did we were quick to repent and get the right words coming out of our mouths.

Most of the people in our church said if they did not know what we were going through they would not have known it by our actions. Most said they did not know if they could go through what we have and handle it like we did. (However, I believe that most of them could)

I don't say any of these previous statements to "brag" in anyway but to share that we are living what I am sharing in this book.
Now back to our earlier verse: Deut 8:2 …. <u>and to test you in order to know what was in your heart, **whether or not you would keep his commands.**</u>

What is the bottom line in why God test's you and wants to

know what is in your heart? He wants to know whether or not you will keep His commands. Again we are back to OBEDIENCE!

In order for you to have success in life you must obey God! We can't get away from obedience! God brings you to those desert places to see if you will STILL obey Him! (He will also take you back there to teach you once again to obey Him if necessary)

Let's look at some examples:

You are in the desert financially. Will you still be faithful in your giving? Or will you say "I can't afford to give"?

You get passed up for a promotion at work. Will you still keep doing your job as unto the Lord? (if you weren't to begin with then there's your answer to why you didn't get the promotion)

Your boyfriend breaks up with you. Will you still trust God to bring you the right boyfriend (a CHRISTIAN one that is). Or will you just hook up with any guy that you are attracted to or gives you any attention? (Disobeying God's Word not to be unequally yoked!)

Several families in your church leave. Will you still obey God and stay where He has planted you? Or will you disobey Him and jump ship with everyone else.
These are just a few examples to consider where you may be tested to see whether you will obey God and what is really in your heart!

You can have a humble heart and walk in complete humility but if there are other heart issues there, your desert experiences can be extended.

So if you find yourself in the desert and have taken care of pride then I would look deep into my heart and see what the Lord is looking for as He probes around! Trust me, He will probe with His all seeing eye!

The sooner you pass the heart check test, the sooner you can be on your way to dessert!

I will close this chapter with this wonderful verse again from James Chapter 1 and verse 12

***Blessed** is the man **who perseveres under trial**, because when **he has stood the test,** he will receive the crown of life that God has promised to those who love him.*

God says you will be BLESSED when you persevere under trial! Blessed means to be made happy! That means you are enjoying the dessert!

He goes on to say that when you have stood (passed) the TEST you will receive the crown of life that God has promised to those who love Him! God does have a wonderful future both in this life and in life eternal for each and every one of us. But you and I have to do things His way and not ours!

Allow God even now to search your heart and ask Him to reveal anything and everything that is displeasing to Him.

PS 139:23 *Search me, O God, and know my heart; test me and know my anxious thoughts.* ***PS 139:24*** *See if there is any* *offensive way in me, and lead me in the way everlasting.*

If He reveals any offensive ways to you that are in your heart then ask for His forgiveness and cleansing. If necessary ask for a new heart that will be pleasing and obedient to Him! He is more than able to do it!

PS 66:10 *For you, O God, tested us; you refined us like silver.* *PS 66:11 You brought us into prison and laid burdens on our backs. PS 66:12 You let men ride over our heads;* **we went through fire and water, but you brought us to a place of abundance.**

It is worth it to be tested! You will be refined like silver. You may go through fire and water but you will be brought to a place of abundance! That is what I call "First the Desert, then the Dessert"

CHAPTER 5- TO TEACH YOU!

Deut 8:3 - *He humbled you, causing you to hunger and then feeding you with manna, which neither you nor your fathers had known<u>, to teach you that man does not live on bread alone but on every word that comes from the mouth of the LORD.</u>*

The final purpose in the Lord bringing you to the desert is to teach you to live according to His EVERY WORD!

Years ago I preached a message from this verse entitled "What are you living on?"

It is worth repeating here because one reason the Lord will take you to the desert is to teach that the only way to live is to live according to His Word. This goes beyond just simple obedience. This includes faith and trust as well.

Matthew Chapter 4 goes into the story of when Jesus was led by the Spirit into the desert to be tempted by the devil. In verse 4 Jesus quotes from Deuteronomy in telling Satan that *"Man does not live on bread alone, but on every word that comes from the mouth of God.'*

Jesus is saying here that it is not enough to live on what feeds our bodies alone. We need to feed our Spirit as well. We can't live our lives according to the world's standards either, but by God's Word.

That is God's desire for all of mankind. That we don't just live on "bread" (food for our bodies) but that we do feed our spirit as well.

We do that by feeding on God's Word! All of us live on something. All of us live our lives either consuming or being consumed by. Many people live on relationships, and others on careers. Many people live for the next "high" the next business deal to conquer. Many young people live on MTV, or their favorite musical group as well as relationships for the joy, peace and satisfaction that only comes from living on God's Word.

It does not matter whether you are young and old, natural food alone doesn't cut it, the relationships, careers and all of these other things are not what will bring real joy, peace, and satisfaction to your life. It is living according to God's Word that will! When you look at much of society and many in the church, we are sure not missing it where feeding our bodies is concerned, but how many of us feed on God's Word anywhere near as much as we feed our bodies?

Jesus said in **John 10:10** that He came that we may have life and have it more abundantly. Was He talking just about us eating well? No, He was talking about living a prosperous life in every area.

The only way that happens is if we are living more on God's Word then feeding our flesh!

The Lord takes you to the desert to teach you that not only do you need to feed on God's Word but live according to it! **Deuteronomy 8:1** again talks about living and increasing. Do you want to live and increase? Then you must obey God's Word!

How are you going to obey God's Word if you don't know what it says? So many in the church are starving spiritually because they live more feeding their bodies and flesh then they do their spirit!

When you find yourself in the desert and needing help, direction, comfort, I bet you get into the Word then! You often find out just how weak your spirit is and how much you do need God's Word.

Jesus himself told some religious people that they did not know the scriptures or the power of God.

MT 22:29 *Jesus replied, "You are in error because you do not know the Scriptures or the power of God.*

Again it is my desire and I know His, that you as a child of God, knows the scriptures and His power. As much as I love the power of God and want the power of God moving in my life and yours, that alone will not sustain you, that alone will not win your battles and help you obtain the promises of God!

You must be living on every Word that comes from the mouth of God. Whether written or spoken to you by His Spirit!

When Satan comes to tempt you and if you want victory the same way Jesus did, then you must defeat him the same way He did.

That was with the Word of God.
But if you are not living on God's Word you won't know what God's Word says. What you are full of will come out when the pressure from the enemy comes.
I don't want a bunch of hot air coming out of me, but I want to be able to declare as did Jesus 'IT IS WRITTEN"!

What are you living on?

How do you live on God's Word? Is it by hearing the preacher preach 2-3 times a week?

Joshua 1:8 again tells us to meditate day and night on God's Word!

We have no problem feeding our bodies 2-3 times a day and some even more, but yet we feed our spirit once or twice a week and think that will do something.

If I were to ask most people want they want out of life the answer would be success and prosperity. (health and good family relationships are included in that)

Well living on God's Word and doing what it says is the way to a successful and prosperous life!

If we spent even half the time feeding on God's word as we do TV. listening to music, focusing on relationships, pursuing our dream careers etc. I believe all of the things we spend so much time spinning our wheels on, would come right to us!

Matthew 6:33- *But seek first his kingdom and his righteousness, and all these things will be given to you as well.*

In seeking first His kingdom and righteousness we must be putting God's Word first! Do that and the rest will come!

But how many believers do that? What are you living on?

We spend time reading a bunch of spiritual books to better

ourselves, to find answers, to build our faith, to get our healing, to find prosperity etc and yet if they are worth reading at all what must they be full of?

God's Word! We need to read God's Word FIRST then spend time reading the others! (this is an area I was convicted on)

I am spending a lot of time on this because it is important! If we would live on and according to God's Word the way we should then we wouldn't be in the desert as much as we are!

There is a saying you can lead a horse to water but you can't make him drink. Well you can sure make him thirsty so he will want to drink!

So I want to make you hungry today for God's Word, so you begin to live on it like you should!

I am going to include here several scriptures to wet your appetite. I am not going to explain or expound on them You can meditate on them yourself!

God does what He says in His Word!

ISA 55:11 *so is my word that goes out from my mouth: It will not return to me empty, but will accomplish what I desire and achieve the purpose for which I sent it.*

JER 1:12 *The LORD said to me, "You have seen correctly, for I am watching to see that my word is fulfilled."*

PS 105:8 *He remembers his covenant forever, the word he* *commanded, for a thousand generations*

God's Word is true!

PS 33:4 *For the word of the LORD is right and true; he is faithful in all he does.*

PS 119:160 *All your words are true; all your righteous laws are eternal.*

God's Word is flawless! No mistakes!

PS 18:30 *As for God, his way is perfect; the word of the LORD is flawless. He is a shield for all who take refuge in him.*

PR 30:5 *"Every word of God is flawless; he is a shield to those who take refuge in him.*

God's Word helps us live a godly life!

PS 119:9 *How can a young man keep his way pure? By living according to your word.* **PS 119:10** *I seek you with all my heart; do not let me stray from your commands.* **PS 119:11** *I have hidden your word in my heart that I might not sin against you.*

God's Word is Living and Powerful!

HEB 4:12 *For the word of God is living and active. Sharper than any double-edged sword, it penetrates even to dividing soul and spirit, joints and marrow; it judges the thoughts and attitudes of the heart.*

1 Pet 1:23 *For you have been born again, not of perishable seed, but of imperishable, through the living and enduring word of God*

1JN 2:14 *I write to you, fathers, because you have known him who is from the beginning. I write to you, young men, because you are strong, and the word of God lives in you, and you have overcome the evil one.*

Getting back to the purpose in this chapter of the Lord taking us to the desert to teach us. His purpose is for us to come to that place where we realize that we MUST live on and according to God's Word.

Not man's word! Not man's warped way of living, but God's Word!

When you are in the desert God can get your attention.

You are more likely to get into the Bible and feed your spirit out of your desperation and need of answers. But that is not God's plan for you.

His plan is that whether you are in the valley or on the mountain you are living on God's Word! His plan is that just like you feed your body daily that your spirit gets fed as well.

His plan is that you seek His Kingdom first! Many times in our lives we are seeking after other things and putting other things first. Being in the desert helps to get your focus where it needs to be!

So I want to encourage you to feed on God's Word every day.

Build your faith up and make your spirit man strong.

There are some other things that God wants to teach you and often the desert is where you will learn them best.

In the next chapter I will share on the first of these next two topics:

>FAITH then Trust!

CHAPTER 6- "FAITH"

Hebrews 11:6- *And without **faith** it is impossible to please God, because anyone who comes to him must believe that he exists and that he rewards those who earnestly seek him.*

This is a very important verse and if we are to ever enjoy the promises of God must get into our hearts and apply to our lives. It is not enough just to believe that God exists. (Devils do that) We must believe that He rewards those who earnestly seek Him! That means we know that if we seek God and walk in faith, that He will bless us and we will receive the promises of God.

HEB 11:1 <u>*Now faith is being sure of what we hope for and certain of what we do not see.*</u>

What is faith? It is being sure, fully persuaded that what we are hoping for, will happen for us even though we do not currently have or see what we are believing God for. We are CERTAIN it will happen.

Another simple definition of faith is: " to get in agreement with God."

If God said it, I agree with Him, regardless of what I see or am currently experiencing. That is faith.

How does this relate to the desert experiences we go through?

2 Cor 5:7 <u>*"We live by faith, not by sight."*</u>

We are to live by faith and not by what we see. What we see is temporary and subject to change. We are to see into the unseen with eyes of faith.

2 Corinthians 4:18- *So we fix our eyes not on what is seen, but on what is unseen. For what is seen is temporary, but what is unseen is eternal.*

In a real desert people often see what they call a "MIRAGE". They think they see "water" or something else and as they get closer to it, they discover it was a mirage and not really there. Their mind and eyes have played tricks on them.

Relate this to us as children of God called to live by faith. What we see with our natural eyes is only temporary and will change.

If we are walking by faith and not sight then we won't get sidetracked, frustrated, discouraged or moved in any way by what we see with our natural eyes. We will stay focused on what God has promised us and keep our eyes fixed on the DESSERT!

God takes us to the desert times to learn faith and to grow in our faith. The desert times are where we will be tested to see if we are going to live by what we see or not.

As stated earlier, if we are in the desert and were to look at our financial situation it is a mess. If we are to look at the loved ones we are praying for to accept Christ they are more rebellious then ever against God. If we were to look at the direction our church is going, it is not what God has showed us concerning His vision for it.

The list can go on and on. When you are in the desert you are put in a position to where you must learn to walk by faith and not sight or you will stay there for a long, long time. We as children must learn to live by faith in God in every area of our lives. The desert is one place where we will learn that.

As I shared in an earlier chapter I had thought that I was living by faith and I found out that was not the case.

Back when I had my business and was making all that money, I gave thanks to God and believed that I had faith in Him concerning all things. I discovered I did not. My faith was in the business and the money it supplied. I borrowed money for anything I wanted because I "knew" I could afford to pay it all back because "the business" would bring it in!

I said God was blessing the business etc but my faith was really not In Him like it should have been, but in the business. When I got stripped of the business and the money it brought in, I saw where my faith was lacking.

The Lord told me I had not really had all my faith in Him as our provider, but in my own abilities and now I was going to learn faith! Ouch!

I spent months reading on faith, listening to great teaching on faith. During this same time we lost everything. I was continually given opportunities to walk by faith or sight.

There were times I did walk by sight. I believed God for the finances to come in personally and in the church. But there were times when it did not come in and I would get upset and let it affect my happiness and decision-making!

One time in particular when I thought I had been standing in faith for our finances, the money did not come in when we needed it. I told God "You have to show me something here. I am believing your Word, standing in faith and nothing is happening. You need to come through for us".

I did not realize what a foolish request that was until the Holy Spirit spoke to me and said: "I have to SHOW you something?" "Are you not to be walking by faith and not sight, and you are telling me to SHOW you something".

It is pretty funny now, although it wasn't at that time. He proceeded to instruct me in the fact that until I learned not to let what I saw and experience affect me then I was not walking in faith and our situation would not turn around.

You see we were in the desert and God was using this time to humble us, test us and teach us. This was not about God not meeting our needs or fulfilling His promises. This was a time He wanted us to learn and grow in faith!

I wish I could say I learned that lesson right away. We went through several months of financial lack. Most of the time I was fine until the next month when we didn't have what we needed and I would get upset and looking for ways to try and fix things.

Finally, I have come to the place where whether we 'SEE" the money come in, or SEE changes or not, it does not affect my moods or actions. It is been a tough lesson to learn.

This is the main thing I have learned and the Lord wants you to learn. If you are walking by faith and not sight, then what you see or are going through will not affect you emotionally, or spiritually.

You will not go running around in the flesh trying to work everything out yourself, or to make things happen the way you want. The faster you learn this and put it into practice the quicker you can get out of the desert and experience the dessert!

Now concerning the Israelites I have stated that only TWO of the original that God delivered from Egypt got to enter the Promised Land. FAITH was the main reason only Joshua and Caleb entered in.

Yes there was the fact that many kept sinning and whining, griping and complaining. But the lack of FAITH was the main reason. Read the next several verses. It is very important that you understand the importance of faith and the part it plays in you receiving all that God has for you. God rewards the faithful!

NU 13:1 *The LORD said to Moses, 2 "Send some men <u>to explore the land of Canaan, which I am giving to the Israelites.</u> From NU 13:3 each ancestral tribe send one of its leaders." So at the LORD's command Moses sent them out from the Desert of Paran. All of them were leaders of the Israelites.*

The Lord said to send men to explore the land He was GIVING them. There are many promises that God has given us.
That does not mean they will just drop in our lap. In the same way the Israelites often had to fight and persevere to receive what God had for them you must do the same.

NU 13:21 *So they went up and explored the land from the Desert of Zin as far as Rehob, toward Lebo Hamath.*

NU 13:26 They came back to Moses and Aaron and the whole Israelite community at Kadesh in the Desert of Paran. There they reported to them and to the whole assembly and showed them the fruit of the land. 27 They gave Moses this account: "We went into the land to which you sent us, and it does flow with milk and honey! Here is its fruit. 28 But the people who live there are powerful, and the cities are fortified and very large. We even saw descendants of Anak there..

They went by faith to spy out the land. They even came back with some of the "fruit" of the land. Then 10 of 12 "leaders" proceeded to tell how POWERFUL the people were there. (they were doubting what God had told them)

*NU 13:30 Then **Caleb** silenced the people before Moses **and said, "We should go up and take possession of the land, for we can certainly do it."***

Caleb had faith and said that they should go and take possession and was CERTAIN that they could do it!

*NU 13:31 But the men who had gone up with him said, **"We can't attack those people; they are stronger than we are."** 32 And they spread among the Israelites a bad report about the land they had explored. They said, "The land we explored devours those living in it. **All the people we saw there are of great size**. 33 **We saw** the Nephilim there (the descendants of Anak come from the Nephilim). **We seemed like grasshoppers in our own eyes, and we looked the same to them."***

The doubters continued to speak all of their doubt all based on what they "saw" and "felt"

Numbers 14:6- <u>**Joshua** son of Nun **and Caleb**</u> son of Jephunneh, who were among those who had explored the land, tore their clothes ⁷ and <u>**said**</u> to the entire Israelite assembly, <u>**"The land we passed through and explored is exceedingly good.** ⁸ **If the LORD is pleased with us, he will lead us into that land, a land flowing with milk and honey, and will give it to us.**</u> ⁹ Only do not rebel against the LORD. And do not be afraid of the people of the land, because we will swallow them up. <u>**Their protection is gone, but the LORD is with us. Do not be afraid of them."**</u>

Joshua and Caleb were men of faith. They were not discouraged by any powerful people they saw. They saw passed them with eyes of faith. They saw that the land was EXCEEDINGLY GOOD! They knew that if the Lord was pleased with them (God is pleased by faith) that He would lead them into the land and give it to them! They KNEW God was with them and that they had nothing to fear!

THAT is FAITH!!

NU 14:10 But the whole assembly talked about stoning them. Then the glory of the LORD appeared at the Tent of Meeting to all the Israelites. ¹¹ <u>**The LORD said**</u> to Moses, <u>**"How long will these people treat me with contempt? How long will they refuse to believe in me, in spite of all the miraculous signs I have performed among them**</u>? ¹² I will strike them down with a plague and destroy them, but I will make you into a nation greater and stronger than they."

God was angry at the lack of faith! He said the people were treating Him with contempt! He said they were refusing to believe in Him! (lack of faith) In their case God had performed many miraculous signs. They had SEEN what God was capable of doing for them and still refused to walk in faith! (Except for Josuah and Caleb)

NU 14:20 *The LORD replied, "I have forgiven them, as you asked. 21 Nevertheless, as surely as I live and as surely as the glory of the LORD fills the whole earth, 22* **not one of the men who saw my glory and the miraculous signs I performed in Egypt and in the desert but who disobeyed me and tested me ten times--** *23* **not one of them will ever see the land I promised on oath to their forefathers.** *No one who has treated me with contempt will ever see it. 24 But* **because my servant Caleb has a different spirit and follows me wholeheartedly, I will bring him into the land he went to, and his descendants will inherit it.**

Numbers 14:30- *Not one of you will enter the land I swore with uplifted hand to make your home, except Caleb son of Jephunneh and Joshua son of Nun.*

Numbes 14:38- *Of the men who went to explore the land, only Joshua son of Nun and Caleb son of Jephunneh survived.*

What was the result? Not one who saw (experienced) all that God did and still walked in unbelief entered the Promised Land!

Joshua and Caleb because they had a different spirit (a spirit of faith) and followed God wholeheartedly (with all of their hearts) entered the Promised Land.

If YOU want to leave the desert and enjoy all that God has promised you then you must become men and women of faith! Men and Women that are not swayed by what they see! Men and Women who do not allow what they see or experience to deter them from what God has promised you. Men and Women that KNOW that God is with you and will not fail you!

How do we become people of faith?

God has given each of us a measure of faith. (Romans 12:3) and faith comes by the continual hearing of God's Word.

Romans 10:17- *Consequently, faith comes from hearing the message, and the message is heard through the word of Christ.*

Our faith grows in part by continually feeding on God's Word. Remember, "What are you living on"?

But faith without works is dead. You must put your faith to work!

JAS 2:18 *But someone will say, "You have faith; I have deeds." Show me your faith without deeds, and __I will show you my faith by what I do.__*

James 2:26 *As the body without the spirit is dead, so __faith without deeds is dead.__*

How you become people of faith is that you continually feed on God's Word and take what measure of faith you have and then begin to put it to work. Begin to believe the promises of God and act on it!

Step out in faith and begin to DO what God has told you to do and called you to do! There is no other way! Jesus often rebuked the disciples for their "little faith", and even "no faith". Once they asked Him to increase their faith. He did not! He just told them what they could do with even a mustard seed of faith.

So take what faith you have wherever you are and the Lord will honor it! Faith at any degree pleases God and causes Him to reward your diligence!

Get Faith and Get the DESSERT!

Concerning the desert, this is the place where your faith will be tested and you will be taught. When things are going your way and you are on the mountaintop it does not take faith. Since God is more concerned about your spiritual growth and maturity He will take you to those desert times to give you opportunities to grow your faith!

One last scripture in this chapter on FAITH:

Mark 9:23- *" If you can'?" said Jesus.* **"Everything is possible for him who believes."**

Jesus said that EVERYTHING is possible for him who believes! Do you BELIEVE that?

CHAPTER 7 " TRUST"

PROVERBS 3:5 *Trust in the LORD with all your heart and lean not on your own understanding;* *PR 3:6* *in all your ways acknowledge him, and he will make your paths straight.*

Another important lesson the Lord wants to teach us that often requires a desert experience is TRUST!

We are told in the above verse to Trust in the Lord with ALL of our hearts! We are told to not lean on our own understanding. We are told that if we do that as well as acknowledge Him in ALL of our ways He will make our paths straight (direct our paths) If we were to automatically do all of that life would be a lot easier. The fact is we often do not TRUST with ALL of our hearts and we often do lean on our own understanding. The desert will help us fix that! Ha!

Many people often think that "faith" and "trust" is the same thing. They are not! In the last chapter I shared some on what faith is.

In this chapter I will share to the best of my ability what trust is and why we need it!

Trust in the simplest definition is to **"full rely on God!"**

Faith is agreeing with God and believing that God will do for you what He said He would do. Trust is relying on God to do it and letting Him do His part!

Trust is you continuing in faith while waiting for the promises of God to come through. Trust is you not relying on your understanding, but knowing that God knows what He is doing and will bring about all that He said He would. Trust is you not trying to "fix" situations that God has told you to trust Him in. Trust is you not trying to figure out: "How God"? When God"? Trust is "letting go and letting God"

It is important that we learn to trust God. Moses and Aaron did not enter the Promised Land because of their lack of trust!

NU 20:12 *But the LORD said to Moses and Aaron, "Because you did not trust in me enough to honor me as holy in the sight of the Israelites, you will not bring this community into the land I give them."*

Those of us that are leaders especially must learn this lesson!

When the Lord brought the Israelites out of Egypt and rescued them from the Egyptian Army they began to trust the Lord.

EX 14:29 *But the Israelites went through the sea on dry ground, with a wall of water on their right and on their left.* **30** *That day the LORD saved Israel from the hands of the Egyptians, and Israel saw the Egyptians lying dead on the shore.* **31** *And when the Israelites saw the great power the LORD displayed against the Egyptians, the people feared the LORD and put their trust in him and in Moses his servant.*

Going back to the Israelites when the 12 were sent to spy the land. They did not trust in the Lord and this was a cause as well of them not leaving the desert and getting their dessert!

DT 1:29 *Then I said to you, "Do not be terrified; do not be afraid of them. 30 The LORD your God, who is going before you, will fight for you, as he did for you in Egypt, before your very eyes, 31 and in the desert. There you saw how the LORD your God carried you, as a father carries his son, all the way you went until you reached this place." DT 1:32* **In spite of this, you did not trust in the LORD your God,**

In the following verse God has told them to go and take possession of the land He has given them! They still don't trust Him!

DT 9:23 *And when the LORD sent you out from Kadesh Barnea, he said,* **"Go up and take possession of the land I have given you."** *But* **you rebelled against the command of the LORD your God. You did not trust him or obey him.** *24 You have been rebellious against the LORD ever since I have known you.*

Several times in scripture the Lord came through for the Israelites as well as providing their needs. Still they would not trust Him and always went back to doubt and unbelief.
Do not follow their example. I am sure all of us have had several times the Lord has come through for us.

But yet how many times when this giant is bigger do we wonder if we can really trust Him to come through again? How many times do we think "yes God did it last time, but maybe I need to help him out this time"? That is not trust! We are to trust God with ALL of our heart! That means no wavering, no doubting or trying to "help God out".

Too many times trust is put in other things then the Lord!

ISA 31:1 *Woe to those who go down to Egypt for help, who rely on horses, who trust in the multitude of their chariots and in the great strength of their horsemen, but do not look to the Holy One of Israel, or seek help from the LORD.*

Don't go to "Egypt" (the world) for help! Don't put your trust in man's methods! Look to the Holy One! Seek help from the Lord!

God's Word is full of promises and what trusting in the Lord will do for us!

PS 9:10 *Those who know your name will trust in you, for you, LORD, have never forsaken those who seek you.*

He will not forsake you so you can trust in Him!

PS 22:4 *In you our fathers put their trust; they trusted <u>and you delivered them</u>.* **PS 22:5** *They cried to you <u>and were saved; in you they trusted and were not disappointed.</u>*

God will not forsake those who trust in Him! He will deliver and save them! You will not be disappointed! (That is good to know when we are in the desert!) The next verses tell us what God will do when we trust, but also give an example of what we should do to demonstrate our trust in Him.

PS 37:5 *Commit your way to the LORD; <u>trust in him and he will do this:</u>* Ps *37:6* <u>*He will make your righteousness shine*</u>

like the dawn, the justice of your cause like the noonday sun.

This is how you show you are trusting in the Lord:

PS 37:7 *Be still before the LORD and wait patiently for him; do not fret when men succeed in their ways, when they carry out their wicked schemes.*

If you are full trusting in the Lord then you will BE STILL before Him. That means you aren't freaking out and trying to figure everything out! Running all over the place to everybody for help!

Next is says that you wait PATIENTLY for HIM! This is one of main ways you know you are trusting in the Lord. When you can wait patiently for Him to come through! As I shared before I am getting much better at patience and waiting on Him!

Finally it says DO NOT FRET! That means DO NOT WORRY! You can't be worrying and trusting at the same time.

In Matthew 6:31 Jesus said *"So do not worry, saying, `What shall we eat?' or `What shall we drink?' or `What shall we wear?'* ^{32} *For the pagans run after all these things, and your heavenly Father knows that you need them.*

He is saying TRUST ME I know what you need and will meet your needs if you give me first place in your life. (verse 33) If you are saying "What shall we eat, drink, wear, do, then you are not trusting! Jesus said the pagans RUN after all these things.

The one who trusts is still before the Lord. The one who trusts waits patiently on the Lord. The one who trusts does not worry!

Jesus says in JN 14:1 *"Do not let your hearts be troubled. Trust in God; trust also in me.*

I believe learning to trust in the Lord is one the most difficult things to learn. All of our lives we have put our trust in people and they have let us down. So then we are told to put our trust in a God that we have never seen and then we have situations where things don't always go the way we want and then we feel the Lord has let us down. The Lord will not and has not let you down. He sees the big picture and will work everything out for your good. We just don't see it all from His perspective. If we knew and saw it all, there would be no need for faith or trust and God requires both from us. There is no better place to learn them both then in the desert!

It takes faith to trust. That is why you need to build up your faith first, and then trust comes.

Trust comes from the relationship. I trust in certain people because I have a relationship with them and have learned over time that I can trust them. It is the same way with the Lord. You need to be in a personal relationship with Him and over time you will learn that He can be trusted.

Obviously learning many of the scriptures that talk about trust and as well as His faithfulness will help. Trust does not come over night but it is something that you must learn if you want to leave the desert and partake of the dessert!

Paul prayed an awesome prayer in Romans 15:13 when he

prayed: ***May the God of hope fill you with all joy and peace as you trust in him***, *so that you may overflow with hope by the power of the Holy Spirit.*

He is asking that God would fill you with ALL JOY AND PEACE <u>as you trust in Him</u>. I read that and think about when we are in those desert places. When I need more joy and I need more peace. Those will come as you trust in Him!

Another way you can come to that place of knowing that you can fully rely on God is to have an understanding of His love for you!

If you really know just how much He loves you and all that entails, you will trust Him!

I ministered a message in my church called "No Greater Love"

Here is a portion of that message: Concerning God's love we are familiar with many of the scriptures that speak about God's love but I want to share some of them again.

John 3:16- *"For God **so loved** the world that he gave his one and only Son, that whoever believes in him shall not perish but have eternal life.*

For God SO LOVED! He SO LOVES YOU! Think of the magnitude of that statement alone! He so loves you!

Rom 5:8- *But **God demonstrates his own love for us in this**: While we were still sinners, Christ died for us.*

Before you were even born, Christ died for you and purchased your salvation. God demonstrates His Love for you. There is no greater love than a love that so loves you. There is no greater love than a love that is demonstrated for you. There is no greater love then the love of a God that gave up His one and only Son to die for you!

There is no greater love than the love of your Heavenly Father!

RO 8:37 *No, in all these things we are more than conquerors through him who loved us. 38 For I am convinced that neither death nor life, neither angels nor demons, neither the present nor the future, nor any powers, 39 neither height nor depth, nor anything else in all creation, will be able to separate us from the love of God that is in Christ Jesus our Lord.*

I have often declared and preached that we are "More Than Conquerors"! But why are we more than conquerors? Because of His love for us and the fact that NOTHING can separate us from God' Love!

I have said it before, but will say it again; **NOTHING can separate you from God's love**. There is nothing you can do to make Him love you more and there is nothing you will do to cause Him to love you less!

1 Corinthians 13:8 tell us that " Love never fails".
God's love for you NEVER FAILS. That means because of God's love for you He will never fail you either! You can trust Him not to let you down!

You need to know that God loves you SO MUCH and that

NOTHING can separate you from His love! You need to know that His love will never fail and that He loves you unconditionally. If you will really open up your heart and receive His love and comprehend just how much God loves you then trusting In Him will come much easier.

Remember 1 Corinthians 13? We call it the "Love Chapter". Part of it says that **"Love always trusts"!** If you really love the Lord in return then you need to learn to always trust Him!

I want to encourage as I close out this chapter:

TRUST in the Lord with all your heart and He will direct your path right out of the desert and into the dessert!

CHAPTER 8   "PERSISTENCE"

Hebrews 6:12- *We do not want you to become lazy, but to imitate those who through faith and patience inherit what has been promised.*

The last topic I am going to share that I believe the Lord wants to teach us in the desert is PERSISTENCE!

It is important to be humbled, to be tested, to grow in faith and trust but you also have to learn to be persistent if you want to receive all that God has for you!

In Hebrews it speaks of those who through FAITH AND PATIENCE inheriting what had been promised.

Persistence is just that. Operating in faith and patience until you receive the promises! Persistence is not quitting, not backing down, not turning around but being determined that no matter how long it takes or no matter what I have to go through I am getting mine!

I can not tell you how many times this following scripture has been spoken from my pulpit but it is so true and so needed in the body of Christ!

Galatians 6:9- *Let us not become weary in doing good, for at the proper time we will reap a harvest if we do not give up.*

God has the proper time when you will receive all that He has for you. But you will not receive it if you give up! You have to be persistent! You have to KEEP DOING GOOD even while in the desert and you don't feel like it!

You keep Praising God daily! You keep forgiving those who offend you! You keep meditating on His Word day and night! You keep giving financially! You keep walking in love! (by the way don't forget that "faith works by love"!

You keep keeping on and you will leave the desert and enjoy the dessert!

Too many people in the church want the easy life. Everything else in life is "fast"! Fast Food, Microwave Ovens, High Speed Internet. Tanning Booths! But God does not see time as we do and is in no hurry! (in case you haven't figured that out yet)

Because of this mentality Christians give up to quick and with little fight when what they believe God for doesn't come in their time frame!

Well guess what? God will take you to the desert to learn to be persistent!

There is a word that for years I just kind of ignored and didn't give it much mind. I guess I figured if I did that then I wouldn't have to experience it or need it. WRONG ANSWER!

That word is LONGSUFFERING!
However, it is a biblical word! It means to suffer long! (don't try and bind the devil over me it won't work)
Longsuffering is translated "Patience" in the New International Version but is used in the Kings James version.

The words are interchangeable but look at the word. Think about what it means. There will be times in your life that you may have to suffer through some things for a long period of time.

That is when you need to have longsuffering or patience!

I can think of no better place again then the desert! So in having persistence again it goes back to having faith and patience! It means you are willing to suffer long if you have to. But you will enter your promised land!

There is a parable that Jesus told about a woman and her persistence.

LK 18:1 *Then Jesus told his disciples a parable to show them that **they should always pray and not give up**. 2 He said: "In a certain town there was a judge who neither feared God nor cared about men. 3 **And there was a widow in that town who kept coming to him with the plea,** `Grant me justice against my adversary.'* LK 18:4 *"For some time he refused. But finally he said to himself, `Even though I don't fear God or care about men, 5 yet **because this widow keeps bothering me, I will see that she gets justice**, so that she won't eventually wear me out with her coming!' "* LK 18:6 *And the Lord said, "Listen to what the unjust judge says. 7 And **will not God bring about justice for his chosen ones, who cry out to him day and night? Will he keep putting them off?** 8 **I tell you, he will see that they get justice, and quickly.** However, when the Son of Man comes, will he find faith on the earth?"*

The moral of that story is that God is not unjust! If an unjust judge would answer a woman's request due to her persistence, how much more will God for us that show persistence!
Getting back to our main story concerning the Israelites and those who left the desert for the dessert. Joshua and Caleb in

part were the only ones who entered in because of their persistence!

Yes they had faith! Yes they trusted in God and proved it time and time again. But they were also persistent!

Moses dies and Joshua had to take over leading the rest of the crowd! There were battles to be fought, city walls to be torn down. That all took persistence!

Think about this. Joshua's "mentor" Moses, was not permitted to enter the Promised Land and had died. Every one else of the original crew had died and was not permitted to enter in.(except for Caleb) They had to take over and lead the new generation in. That is a lot to deal with and work through. But they did it!

That is persistence! God had promised them lands and victories in battles but they still had to fight! They still had enemies to conquer! They did fight every battle, did persist and left the desert and received the dessert!

Likewise, God has promised you lands and victory over every battle but you too still have enemies to fight.

I understand Satan is an enemy and we are at warfare with him. I understand he is defeated and we have the victory.
He still keeps coming and does still deceive many a believer.
As much time as we may spend fighting the good fight in winning the battles he may bring, our biggest enemy can still be SELF!

Think about what you have learned in this book. It is about us getting the pride out of self. It is God testing you to see what is in your heart! It is you having to get faith, and trust. In all of that it is you having to get victory over self!

That all takes persistence! It does not happen over night! You will live with you until your spirit leaves your body to go be with the Lord! So realize that often times the enemy is not just the devil and KNOW that God is not your enemy either. But often times it is your own flesh you have to get the victory over!

In everything in life it takes persistence to win! You can ask the majority of self made millionaires or business owners. They had to persist through many obstacles to get where they are and to get what they got! Successful sports figures and entertainers all had to persist through much opposition. But they did not quit!

Women have persisted through miscarriages and the emotional pain that causes, to finally get to have a baby.

Many a pastor has had to persist through many obstacles to have a thriving church.

Missionaries persist through being away from home and family. They persist through lacking many of the comforts that this country affords them. Many persist through sickness, and financial struggles all for the prize of fulfilling the call of God on their lives. They persist as well to know that one day they will hear those words we all long to hear "well done good and faithful servant".

What about all of those who have been murdered while leaving the comforts of home to minister Jesus to the lost and dying across the world? It is a slap in their face and the memory of the untold faces of all of those who have been martyred for the cause of Christ, for any of us who never give up anything compared to what they have, to whine, gripe, complain and quit!

We all will have desert experiences at some point in our lives for all the reasons I have shared in this book. The only way you will leave the desert and enjoy the dessert is if you persist through it all!

Let's follow the example of Paul again who said:

2 Timothy 4:7 *I have fought the good fight, I have finished the race, I have kept the faith.* ^{8} *Now there is in store for me the crown of righteousness, which the Lord, the righteous Judge, will award to me on that day--and not only to me, but also to all who have longed for his appearing.*

I know we read these two verses earlier and I addressed them but they bear repeating. They refer to Paul's persistence!
He fought the good fight! He finished the race. He kept the faith! Because he did persist then he knew he had a reward waiting for him.

1CO 9:24 *Do you not know that in a race all the runners run, but only one gets the prize? Run in such a way as to get the prize.* ^{25} *Everyone who competes in the games goes into strict training. They do it to get a crown that will not last; but we do it to get a crown that will last forever.* ^{26} *Therefore I do not run like a man running aimlessly; I do not fight like a man beating the air.* ^{27} *No, I beat my body and make it my slave so that after I have preached to others, I myself will not be disqualified for the prize.*

Paul again is speaking of persistence! Not every one will run or persist through to get the prize. It takes discipline and determination and again getting victory over "self". Paul said he beat his body and made it a slave so that he would not be disqualified for the prize! That again is persistence in action!

I encourage you to keep your eyes on the prize as well! Your prize may be healing. It may be financial breakthrough. It may be seeing your family coming to Christ. It may be the fulfillment of the ministry vision God has given you. It does not matter what your prize is. What matters is that you persist until you get it! Don't stay in the desert. Persist through every "affliction" and go for the dessert no matter how long it takes! It will be worth it all!

CHAPTER 9   HOW TO RESPOND IN THE DESERT.

I have already discussed some of the things throughout this book that relate to his chapter but some need to be repeated so you may see some of the again. If you want to leave the desert and enjoy the dessert then there are proper ways to respond if you want to enjoy the Promised Land.

One of the first things you must determine to do when you find you are in a desert experience is to **determine that above everything you want God's will above your own!**

He is to be our master and our Lord. If He has brought you to, or allowed you to go to this desert then there is a reason for it.

He wants you to be humbled, tested or taught! You need to discover which of any or all that it is. Then regardless of how uncomfortable you may be you need to accept the fact that this is about God's will for me not my own. This is an area where we can really miss it. We think we know what God's plan for us is. Many of us would say "What I am going through now is not what I want and I don't believe it can be God's will for me." Well for a season it may be and you need to accept that!

What did Jesus tell us to pray in what we commonly call The Lord's Prayer"?

Matthew 6:10 *your kingdom come, **your will be done** on earth as it is in heaven.* That's right! We are to pray for HIS will to be done on earth.

What did Jesus pray when He was in the garden before He knew He was going to be arrested, beaten and crucified?

MT 26:36 *Then Jesus went with his disciples to a place called Gethsemane, and he said to them, "Sit here while I go over there and pray." ³⁷ He took Peter and the two sons of Zebedee along with him, **and he began to be sorrowful and troubled**. ³⁸ Then he said to them, **"My soul is overwhelmed with sorrow to the point of death.** Stay here and keep watch with me." MT 26:39 Going a little farther, he fell with his face to the ground and prayed, "My Father**, if it is possible, may this cup be taken from me. Yet not as I will, but as you will**." MT 26:40 Then he returned to his disciples and found them sleeping. "Could you men not keep watch with me for one hour?" he asked Peter. ⁴¹ "Watch and pray so that you will not fall into temptation. The spirit is willing, but the body is weak." MT 26:42 He went away a second time and prayed, **"My Father, if it is not possible for this cup to be taken away unless I drink it, may your will be done."***

You can tell from reading from this story that it was not pleasurable for Jesus. He was sorrowful and troubled. His soul was overwhelmed with sorrow to the point of death. He prayed that if it was possible, if there were any other way for this cup to be taken away from him. But He still through His anguish and sorrow declared that He wanted GOD'S WILL.

How many of us going through the desert can say that or even pray that? The fact of the matter is until you can place your will below God's will, you won't be leaving the desert any time soon.

PS 40:8 *I desire to do your will, O my God; your law is within my heart."*

Is it your desire to do God's will? It must be!

The Psalmist prayed in **PS 143:***10* *"<u>Teach me to do your will</u>, for you are my God; may your good Spirit lead me on level ground."*

The Lord will teach you to do His will and often it will happen while you are in the desert. Many people will be doing their own thing fulfilling their will and the Lord will take them to the desert to get their attention and teach them. We are more willing to listen to the Lord when we are in an uncomfortable environment. We are more willing to listen to the Lord too because we are usually seeking His face in prayer more wanting to know "what's going on?" "Why is THIS happening to me?" The Lord now has your attention and will let you know what His will is for you.

Now I am not saying that the Lord always takes you to the desert to get your attention or to impress upon you what His will is.

What I am saying is that if keep ignoring Him when He is speaking or impressing upon you what direction He desires for you to go then He can and will take you to the desert. So if you find yourself in the desert be open real quick to hear and to submit to God's will. We often think we have God figured out. We often think we know what is best for us and what God's will is for us. That is not the case.

ISA 55:8 *"For my thoughts are not your thoughts, neither are* *your ways my ways, "declares the LORD.* **ISA 55:9** *"As the heavens are higher than the earth, so are my ways higher than your ways and my thoughts than your thoughts.*

God is GOD and the way He thinks and the way we think is often not on the same page. His way of doing things and our ways of doing things are often not the same. That is why we need His thoughts and His ways.

When you are in the desert one of the first things you need to accept is that at this time you are there and this is God's will for you. You need to learn why He has you there.

God is the POTTER we are the clay. He is molding us into who He wants us to be!

ISA 29:16 *You turn things upside down, as if the potter were thought to be like the clay! Shall what is formed say to him who formed it, "He did not make me"? Can the pot say of the potter, "He knows nothing"?*

ISA 45:9 *"Woe to him who quarrels with his Maker, to him who is but a potsherd among the potsherds on the ground. Does the clay say to the potter, `What are you making?*
Romans 9:21 *But who are you, O man, to talk back to God? "Shall what is formed say to him who formed it, `Why did you make me like this?'"* **21** *Does not the potter have the right to make out of the same lump of clay some pottery for noble purposes and some for common use?*

NOT MY WILL- BUT YOURS BE DONE!

The next proper response is to control your tongue!

I already shared some; but whining, gripping and complaining will not help you in any way!

I am not saying just your "positive confession" will get you out of the desert. It will help you control your tongue, build on your faith and bring about the blessing of God. It is a fact that we will eat the fruit of our lips and that the power of death and life is in the tongue. But just speaking God's Word won't bring about a quick end to your desert. (Not if there are things He is wanting to teach you or test you on.)

I am again addressing all of the negative talk (complaining) that we do too often when going through a test. It does nothing but prove our need to be there because what is coming out of our mouth is ultimately from what is in out heart.

The Lord did so much for the Israelites in rescuing them from Pharoah and the bondage they were in while in Egypt. He kept them healthy, provided for them, protected then and delivered them but they always found something to complain about.

However, most of the Israelites grumbled and complained:

EX 17:3 *But the people were thirsty for water there, and they grumbled against Moses. They said, "Why did you bring us up out of Egypt to make us and our children and livestock die of thirst?"*
NU 14:1 *That night all the people of the community raised their voices and wept aloud. 2 All the Israelites grumbled against Moses and Aaron, and the whole assembly said to them, "If only*

we had died in Egypt! Or in this desert! ³ *Why is the LORD bringing us to this land only to let us fall by the sword? Our wives and children will be taken as plunder. Wouldn't it be better for us to go back to Egypt?"* ⁴ *And they said to each other, "We should choose a leader and go back to Egypt."*

Yes it says the grumbled against Moses or Moses and Aaron. But they were God's messengers doing what God told them to do in leading the Israelites out of bondage and into freedom. All they could do was grumble and complain.

NU 11:1 *Now the people complained about their hardships in the hearing of the LORD, and when he heard them his anger was aroused. Then fire from the LORD burned among them and consumed some of the outskirts of the camp.*

I don't think the Lord is pleased with complaining. Having Him be angry with you for it is not going to speed up the process of your departure from the desert!

Instead be like Joshua and Caleb and speak faith!

Be like David who prayed the following:

PS 141:3 *Set a guard over my mouth, O LORD; keep watch over the door of my lips.*

He asked the Lord to set a guard over his mouth. Now we know the Lord will let you speak whatever you want out of your mouth but by His Holy Spirit He can sure make you aware of what you are saying. David knew the importance of watching what came out of his mouth. It is important that we do as well. Especially while going through situations we don't like.

This is what you should be doing with your tongue:

PS 35:28 *My tongue will speak of your righteousness and of your praises all day long.* He says he will speak of God's righteousness and praises ALL DAY LONG!

David said in **PS 34:1** "I will extol the LORD at all times; his praise will always be on my lips."

He said he would extol (bless, exalt, lift up) the Lord at ALL TIMES. Not just when he felt like it or when things were going his way. ALL TIMES! In the desert you need to be exalting the Lord!

We all are familiar with Paul and Silas in the prison. They were beaten and arrested for preaching the gospel and casting a devil out of a girl. They did not gripe and complain but they prayed and sang hymns to God and an angel came and broke them out of prison. In the process the jailer and his entire family came to Christ.

Was it worth it for an entire family to be saved for Paul and Silas to spend some time in prison? I don't believe that the Lord had to send them to jail, or that He has to send you to the desert for others to come to Christ. But if you will respond the way you should while you are there, then God can win souls through it!

Much of all of what I am sharing in this book is about your perspective and attitude. If you will have a positive attitude and see from God's perspective then things will go much better for you and you will often get to the dessert much faster then if you have a bad attitude about everything you are going through.

There is a good friend of ours who attends our church and is at the writing of this book going through a desert experience. As I share some of her life experiences with you I believe it will amaze you that not only is she still sane, but is serving God and wants nothing less than to please God with all of her heart and to be used of God to bring others into the Kingdom. Most people could probably not even imagine all of this happening to any one person much less themselves. Many people probably would not even still be serving the Lord and have quit serving Him over less. But this woman knows the strength, mercy and love of her God and is still running her race.

Several years ago Donna's brother who was her pastor, fell off the church roof and ended up dying. A few months later while she was still grieving from that loss, her children were in a car accident with her husband driving, and two of her children died. (A boy and a girl.) The funerals were right before Christmas. That would have done many a believer in. Several years later she divorced her husband who was a drunk, drug addict and adulterer. (he left her for another woman).While this was going on she found out she had cancer. She had surgery and thank God has been cancer free ever since. Donna had also battled depression for several years while still serving the Lord. Several years ago at a women's meeting at another church Donna received prayer by a woman that knew nothing about her and the Lord set her free from depression as well as much of her past hurts.

You would think she had been through enough for one life time.

Through other things out of her control she went through a financial desert as well. She lost a car and eventually lost her home. She and a son had to move into an apartment.

Right now she is still serving God with all of her heart. Nearly every service she is on her knees or face before God in worship. She has told me how much she has learned and grown these past several years in our church. Yet she is still going through another battle that none of us would want. As her pastor I am as proud as can be. Here is a woman that has lost so much in life but has learned much. Here is a woman that has stood when many a "man" would have given up. Here is a woman that when GOD delivers her from the desert will once again experience more of the blessings of God then many would even hope to. Donna has been much of my inspiration in writing this book.

I shared all of that to say this. Through it all she has said "NOT MY WILL, BUT HIS BE DONE!" Through it all she has continued to PRAISE GOD and THANK GOD for His goodness!

Can you? Would you? Will you?

She has not whined, gripped and complained like most people would. Oh yes she has been down, discouraged, and wondered why? But she always gets back up and knows where here strength comes from. She knows there is no better way then God's way. She knows there is no way out but to praise your way out!

When God gets through with her in this desert experience she will be so thankful once again for all that God has done in her, for her, and through her. It is my desire for everyone reading this book to become all that God wants you to be and to experience all that God has for you as well.

Unfortunately we will most likely have to go through some desert experiences for that to happen. But if you will accept whatever God's will for you is as well as control your tongue you will experience all of the blessings God has for you!

There is one last thing in this chapter I need to discuss in how to respond while in the desert. **You must control your thoughts!**

What you think about to a great degree will be what you speak about. What you speak about will bring about what you will experience the most from this point on.
So get your thought life right! If you are continually thinking about all the bad that has happened to you or all that you are going through you will never leave the desert. You will stay down, discouraged and depressed thinking about where you should be, could be or want to be.

You are where you are. Your past is your past. Your mistakes are your mistakes. Time to forget about the past and move on! To do that you must think about victory, about the promises of God, the faithfulness of God and the goodness of God.

PHP 4:8 *Finally, brothers, whatever is true, whatever is noble, whatever is right, whatever is pure, whatever is lovely, whatever is admirable--if anything is excellent or praiseworthy--think about such things.*
Often when people are in the desert they are thinking about how unhappy they are and all they are missing out on. What good does any of that do?

There are plenty of people in the scripture who had tragedies and went through tough times. So you are not alone!

Think on only the things that are going to build you up, restore your hope, increase your faith and bring about your deliverance!

We are told in several places in scripture not to worry. Worry is the same as "taking thought of" If you are worrying you are thinking negatively. Stop it!

Think on the good things! Think about what it will be like when all your needs are met. Think about what it will be like when your relationships are restored and repaired. Think about what it will be like when you are doing the ministry God has called you to. Think about all of the visions and dreams God has given you. Those are the things that will help see you through your desert experiences.

Think about Joseph. God had given him dreams. He got sold into slavery, falsely accused of rape, put into prison, interpreted others dreams and forgot about…but he held onto his dreams and he got delivered from the prison and returned to the palace. The dreams God showed him all came to pass! What do you think kept him going all of those years and through all of his misfortunes?

I guarantee you it sure wasn't thinking about and dwelling on all the bad that had happened to him. He had a dream and he would not let go. I am sure he spent many a moment in prison "thinking" about the day he would be free. Thinking about the day he would be prospering and leading again. The Lord will deliver you as well from whatever desert you are in but you must get your thought life under control!

CHAPTER 10   DESSERT IN THE DESERT

In the last chapter under controlling your tongue I mentioned how we should guard what comes out of our mouth. I shared how we should not be grumbling and complaining, but how David spoke of exalting (blessing) the Lord at all times. In this chapter I want to talk about one of the most important things you can do and should do especially while you are in the desert. If you will do this you can have some dessert even in the desert.

If you will praise God like David said, you can even in the midst of the desert experience have some mighty and powerful encounters with the living God. You can still have health, peace and financial provision in the desert.

It is God's strength and power you will need to get you through some of those deep, dark and lonely times. It is KNOWING that God is there because you feel His presence that will help get you through. It is those tastes of dessert as well that will help keep you going until you get into your Promised Land.

There is nothing I enjoy more then pursuing God's presence and experiencing His Glory in our church and in my life. Nothing compares to it and I would not give up anything for it.

Beyond us giving our lives to the Lord, there is nothing He desires more than our worship! If you give God what He desires He will surely give you what you desire.

PS 37:4 *Delight yourself in the LORD and he will give you the desires of your heart.*

There are various ways to delight in the Lord but one of them is to give Him praise! As you give Him praise He will give you your hearts desire.

Think about it. If you were God and your son or daughter was in the desert. You knew they needed to be there to learn and to grow. But all they did was complain, would you be pleased?

What if they were to give you praise and thank you for who you were and all you had done for them. Would that not make you gleam with pride and joy? Would that not want you to all the more bless them and see them victorious in every area of their life?

Well if you think that way how much more does the Lord? If we would have faith in God and trust Him in every area of our lives as we should then it would not be that difficult to praise Him regardless of what was going on in our lives.

It is an expression of faith to praise God when you don't feel like it everything is going wrong. That is the time you should be giving Him praise!

The Psalms are full of examples of praises from David and I want to share some of them in this chapter to encourage you once again that even in the desert you can have some dessert!

PS 7:17 *I will give thanks to the LORD because of his righteousness and will sing praise to the name of the LORD Most High.*

Why do we give thanks to the Lord and sing praise to His name? He is a righteous God!

PS 16:7 *I will praise the LORD, who counsels me; even at night my heart instructs me.* **PS 16:8** <u>*I have set the LORD always before me. Because he is at my right hand, I will not be shaken.*</u> **PS 16:9** <u>*Therefore my heart is glad and my tongue rejoices; my body also will rest secure*</u>, **PS 16:10** *because you will not abandon me to the grave, nor will you let your Holy One see decay.*

You will not be shaken no matter what you go through in life if you will set the Lord always before you. Focus on Him. Give Him first place in your life. Your heart can be glad and your tongue rejoice and your body can rest secure, knowing He is always there and will not leave you or forsake you!

PS 18:3 <u>*I call to the LORD, who is worthy of praise, and I am saved from my enemies*</u>. **PS 18:4** *The cords of death entangled me; the torrents of destruction overwhelmed me.* **PS 18:5** *The cords of the grave coiled around me; the snares of death confronted me.* **PS 18:6** <u>*In my distress I called to the LORD;I cried to my God for help. From his temple he heard my voice; my cry came before him, into his ears.*</u>

David called to His Lord who is worthy of praise! He felt like death entangled him and destruction was overwhelming but He gave God praise! He was in distress but called to the Lord and God heard his cry for help!

No matter how bad your life may be. No matter how bad you feel or what is happening to you. You can still give God praise. He is worthy! If you do, He will hear and He will answer!

PS 28:6 *Praise be to the LORD, for he has heard my cry for mercy.* *PS 28:7 The LORD is my strength and my shield; my heart trusts in him, and I am helped. My heart leaps for joy and I will give thanks to him in song. PS 28:8 The LORD is the strength of his people, a fortress of salvation for his anointed one.*

The Psalmist acknowledged that God heard his cry for mercy! He said that the Lord IS my STRENGTH and my SHIELD! He said that He TRUSTS in Him and was helped! As his heart leaps for joy He gives thank to the Lord in song. Once again the Lord is the strength of his people and a fortress of salvation.

No matter how low you may get if you will dig deep into your spirit and give God praise He will lift you up! He will be your strength! He will be your shield! He will be your help!

PS 34:2 *My soul will boast in the LORD; **let the afflicted hear and rejoice.** PS 34:3 Glorify the LORD with me; let us exalt his name together. PS 34:4 I sought the LORD, and he answered me; he delivered me from all my fears.*
Are you afflicted? If so then hear and rejoice! Glorify the Lord with me! Let us exalt His name together! If you will the Lord will answer you and deliver you!

PS 42:5 *Why are you downcast, O my soul? Why so disturbed within me? Put your hope in God, for I will yet praise him, my Savior and 6 my God.*
Have you every felt downcast? (depressed) Disturbed within? Then follow David's advice to himself! He spoke to his own self and said to put your hope in God and declared that he would yet

praise His Savior and God! That is some good advice and what I have been wanting to get across to everyone reading this book.

You can count on God! You can bank on God's Word! If you will do what it says you will be victorious. Even when you are down, depressed and disturbed, if you will praise the Lord He will bring you out!

Actually two times in Psalm 42 and in the end of Chapter 43 David repeats the line "why are you downcast, O my soul" etc. (42:5, 42:11 and 43:5).

Why? Obviously he was feeling pretty downcast and the turnaround didn't happen the first time he told himself to put his hope in God! THAT is a lesson to be learned. That tells me not to quit just because nothing changes or I don't "feel" any better. You have to keep hoping, keep believing, keep trusting and keep praising the Lord!

PS 57:1 *Have mercy on me, O God, have mercy on me, for in you my soul takes refuge. I will take refuge in the shadow of your wings until the disaster has passed.* **PS 57:2** *I cry out to God Most High, to God, who fulfills his purpose for me.*

David knew where his soul was to take refuge! He knew what to do until the disaster had passed! He knew God would fulfill His purpose in his life!

PS 57:3 *He sends from heaven and saves me, rebuking those who hotly pursue me; Selah God sends his love and his faithfulness.* **PS 57:4** *I am in the midst of lions; I lie among ravenous beasts-- men whose teeth are spears and arrows,* *whose tongues are sharp swords.* PS 57:5 *Be exalted, O God, above the heavens; let your glory be over all the earth.*

You can know like David that God will send His love and faithfulness to save you. If you will still exalt the Lord even when you feel like you are in the midst of lions and your life is being torn apart, He will deliver you as well!

I so want you to see that our God is worthy of praise and that if you will praise Him in the desert you will get some dessert. He will bless you with His presence, His power and His peace. If you have to get up every day and encourage yourself in the Lord as David did then so be it!

Anybody can praise God and give God thanks when everything is going there way! It takes a special breed to praise Him in the desert. Be that special breed!

Praise Him in the morning! Praise Him in the noontime! Praise Him all day and night!

If you do He will invade your circumstance. Whether your breakthrough or deliverance comes right away or not, He will be there with you in a special way and you will know it!

As I close this chapter I want to leave you with some additional advice. All too often God delivers, God heals, God comes through and people forget about it all too quick. Don't forget what God has done for you. Don't forget where He brought you from! Don't forget where He brought you too. The day will come when you have left the desert and are experiencing the dessert and this is what God's Word reminds you to do:

DT 8:10 <u>*When you have eaten and are satisfied, praise the LORD your God for the good land he has given you.*</u> *11 Be careful that you do not forget the LORD your God, failing to observe his commands, his laws and his decrees that I am giving you this day.*
18 <u>**But remember the LORD your God, for it is he who gives you the ability to produce wealth,**</u> *and so confirms his covenant, which he swore to your forefathers, as it is today.*

The day will come when you have eaten and are satisfied! The day will come when you have entered the good land He has given you. Don't forget to continue to give God thanks and to give God praise! Don't stop obeying His Word. Don't go back to the old way you used to live! Remember the LORD YOUR GOD! It is He that gave you that power to produce the wealth you will one day have!

CHAPTER 11 FINALLY, THE DESSERT

Deut 6:18 Do what is right and good in the LORD'S sight, so that it may go well with you and **you may go in and take over the good land that the LORD promised on oath to your forefathers...**

Deut 8:7- For the LORD your God is bringing you into a good land--a land with streams and pools of water, with springs flowing in the valleys and hills; ^{8} a land with wheat and barley, vines and fig trees, pomegranates, olive oil and honey; ^{9} **a land where bread will not be scarce and you will lack nothing**; a land where the rocks are iron and you can dig copper out of the hills. DT 8:10 **When you have eaten and are satisfied, praise the LORD your God for the good land he has given you.**

As I shared in the first chapter of this book, the Lord has many promises for each and every one of us as His children. He has promised to bring us into a "GOOD LAND". A place where bread will not be scarce and we will lack nothing. A place where we will eat and be satisfied! This is a good place to be. However as I have shared all through this book, to get to that good land we often have to go through the desert.

Once you go through the desert and have been humbled, tested and taught you can expect to enter into the good land and enjoy the dessert! What is the dessert? It is experiencing the blessing of God to where you have all that you need financially. It is where you are walking in health. The dessert is where you are full of joy, peace and walking in victory. The dessert is where life is good, and your ministry is growing and advancing the Kingdom of God.

It is a wonderful place to be!

I want to share one last Biblical account of a man that went through the desert and enjoyed the dessert. That man was Job!

JOB 1:1 *In the land of Uz there lived a man whose name was Job.* <u>***This man was blameless and upright; he feared God and shunned evil.***</u> *² He had seven sons and three daughters, ³ and he owned seven thousand sheep, three thousand camels, five hundred yoke of oxen and five hundred donkeys, and had a large number of servants. He was the greatest man among all the people of the East.*

Here was a man that feared God and shunned evil and lived a blameless life. You can read through the first two chapters of Job and see what happened. But he lost his possessions, servants, children, and animals. Satan also placed sickness on his body.

Job was a man that lost much. After he lost all of these things, his wife wanted him to curse God and die. But he would not. He refused to deny his integrity. I believe Job knew there was to be dessert after the desert. Through the book of Job there are various conversations with different "friends" of his. There is one however that was really encouraging. If you are in the desert let this minister to you as well!

One of Job's friends Bildad the Shuhite said in

JOB 8:5 But if you will look to God and plead with the Almighty, **JOB 8:6** if you are pure and upright, **even now** he will rouse himself on your behalf and **restore you to your rightful place**. **JOB 8:7** **Your beginnings will seem humble, so prosperous will your future be.**

What an awesome word! Bildad told Job that if he would look to God and yes even plead with him, that if Job would live right. That even now God would rouse Himself on Job's behalf and RESTORE HIM TO HIS RIGHTFUL PLACE! Bildad also told Job that his beginnings would seem humble compared to how prosperous his future would be!

God has a rightful place for each of us. That is a place of health, prosperity, joy, peace and victory! God promises to restore you to your rightful place as well!

Job was a wealthy man who lost it all but in the end when he left the desert, he got back double of everything he had lost! That sounds like some good dessert to me!

JOB 42:10 *After Job had prayed for his friends,* ***the LORD made him prosperous again and gave him twice as much as he had before.*** *11 All his brothers and sisters and everyone who had known him before came and ate with him in his house. They comforted and consoled him over all the trouble the LORD had brought upon him, and each one gave him a piece of silver and a gold ring.* **JOB 42:12** ***The LORD blessed the latter part of Job's life more than the first.*** *He had fourteen thousand sheep, six thousand camels, a thousand yoke of oxen and a thousand* *donkeys.* ¹³ *And he also had seven sons and three daughters.* ¹⁴ *The first daughter he named Jemimah, the second Keziah and the third Keren-Happuch.* ¹⁵ *Nowhere in all the land were there found women as beautiful as Job's daughters, and their father granted them an inheritance along with their brothers.* JOB 42:16 *After this, Job lived a hundred and forty years; he saw his children and their children to the fourth generation.* ¹⁷ <u>**And so he died, old and full of years.**</u>

Notice that the Lord made Job prosperous again! He was prosperous before and the Lord did it again with even more! That should be good news for some of you. It is for me! I have been prosperous before and lost it and as of this writing the Lord has blessed me with a business again it is far surpassing the last one!

The Lord blessed the latter part of Job's life MORE than the first! It does not matter what has happened in your past, good or bad. It does not matter what you may be going through right now. God can turn your life around and you can be enjoying the dessert more in the latter part of your life!

Don't look at what you have lost, but look to what you will gain!

Job's story tells me there is hope for each and every one of us. No matter what we go through, no matter what the devil may steal, no matter what we have lost, there will come a day when we will be brought back to our rightful place!

ZEC 9:12 Return to your fortress, O prisoners of hope; <u>**even now I announce that I will restore twice as much to you.**</u>

Some people out of their pain, hopelessness and frustration turn away from the Lord. He says to RETURN TO YOUR FORTRESS! Return to the one who is your refugee, your strength your rock, your redeemer!

If you will, He says that EVEN NOW He will restore twice as much to you!

I am sure most of you have not turned your back on the Lord but you may have backed off on your praise. I encourage you to return to your fortress with your praise! Read the last chapter over and over until you are doing what it says!

If you have walked away from the Lord during your desert experience you must come back to Him. You must allow Him to do in you all that I have shared in this book. If you will He will restore you to your rightful place! He will restore twice as much, if not more to you!

It does not matter how far you have fallen, the Lord will always be there to pick you up. He is merciful, slow to anger and abounding in love. If you have turned away then return to Him, ask for forgiveness and receive all that He has for you.

I John 1:9 *If we confess our sins, he is faithful and just and will forgive us our sins and purify us from all unrighteousness..*

There is no greater love then the love your Heavenly Father has for you. Even though you may go through many afflictions you need to know that He loves you. You may have grieved His heart by your sin, grumbling and complaining. But it is not too late to stop it and turn around.

The Lord has a good land for each and every one of us. He wants you to enjoy it more than I do. But you must go through the desert before you can enjoy the dessert. Keep your focus on the dessert!

See yourself healed!
See yourself prosperous!
See yourself walking in victory!
See yourself being used of God being a witness to others.

What promises of God are you believing for?

See yourself possessing them!
See yourself enjoying the good land!
See with the eyes of faith like Joshua and Caleb!
Let the Lord humble you, test you and teach you.
Trust Him.
Increase your faith.
Persist through the desert.
Give God Praise!

If you do you will one day leave the desert and enjoy the dessert!

I started this book in 2005 and had completed most of it including this chapter, but had not left the desert yet. So I waited until I could share that we are now experiencing the dessert! I can now say we have left the desert and are now experiencing the dessert. After several years of preaching and doing what I have shared in this book the Lord opened up a business for me January of this year, (2011) in the middle of a bad economy with many out of work, and high home foreclosures etc. I am now earning more then I did with the last business and have more people working for me then I did before. We will personally be debt free by the end of this year. But this time my trust and faith is fully in the Lord. He restored and He gets all the glory. Instead of getting in more debt we are going to get out of debt! During famine and the desert we continued serving God faithfully and sowed into the Kingdom and now...the dessert!

Our church had stagnated for past several years but have recently started to experience growth again. This time last year (2010) we were back to meeting with a few people in our basement for services. This after several previous years of having more people, more money and we met in different rented meeting places. Our church has gone through the desert and now the dessert! In November we began meeting at a temporary meeting place on Sundays and we were all rejoicing over that.

But now.. the dessert....

We are in the process of renting a church building that has way more room then we currently need, and is above and beyond anything we could have imagined! Ephesians 3:20 in action!

We are eating the dessert and it is so worth the desert we walked through! We all have grown so much in every area of our lives!

We have in no way "arrived" but are enjoying the blessing and favor of God, as well as what we learned while in the desert.

The dessert is so sweet and worth the wait!

FIRST the desert, THEN the dessert!

PS 66:12... we went through fire and water, but you brought us to a place of abundance.

If I did not end this book with giving those of you reading it an opportunity to give your heart and life to the Lord if you have not already, then this would all be a waste. There is no "dessert" for you unless you are a child of God. You are only His child if you have been born again into His family and Kingdom. We all have sinned and fallen short and need forgiveness of our sin. It is by our acknowledgement of that and by putting our faith and trust in Jesus as our Savior and Lord that we become a child of God. As His child of God we have all rights that come from being an heir of God and joint heir with Jesus. Every promise of God to include eternal life, is available to all who will put their faith in Him and turn their lives over to Him. I encourage you today that if you would like to turn your life over to God or come back to Him if you have strayed, to pray this prayer:

Dear God in heaven, I come to you in the name of Jesus. I acknowledge to You that I am a sinner, and I am sorry for my sins and the life that I have lived; I need your forgiveness. I believe that your only begotten Son Jesus Christ shed His precious blood on the cross at Calvary and died for my sins, and I am now willing to turn from my sin. You said in Romans 10:9 that if we confess the Lord our God and believe in our hearts that God raised Jesus from the dead, we shall be saved. Right now I confess Jesus as my Lord. With my heart, I believe that God raised Jesus from the dead. This very moment I accept Jesus Christ as my own personal Savior and according to His Word, right now I am saved.